Intellectual Property Rights in Frontier Industries

Intellectual Property Rights in Frontier Industries

Software and Biotechnology

Edited by
Robert W. Hahn

AEI-Brookings Joint Center for Regulatory Studies
WASHINGTON, D.C.

Distributed to the Trade by National Book Network, 15200 NBN Way, Blue Ridge Summit, PA 17214. To order call toll free 1-800-462-6420 or 1-717-794-3800. For all other inquiries please contact the AEI Press, 1150 Seventeenth Street, N.W., Washington, D.C. 20036 or call 1-800-862-5801.

Library of Congress Cataloging-in-Publication Data

   Intellectual property rights in frontier industries: software and biotechnology / edited by Robert W. Hahn
       p. cm.
   Includes bibliographical references and index.
   ISBN 0-8447-7191-0 (alk. pbk.)
   1. Software protection—Law and legislation—United States. 2. Biotechnology industries—Law and legislation—United States. 3. Bioinformatics—Software. 4. Intellectual property—Economic aspects. I. Hahn, Robert W. II. Title.

   KF3024.C6157 2005
   346.7304'8—dc22
                                                        2005001413
   ISBN 978-0-8447-7191-5

10 09 08 07 06 05 04   1 2 3 4 5

American Enterprise Institute
1150 17th Street, N.W.
Washington, D.C. 20036

1

Contents

Illustrations

Preface

The appropriate dimensions of protection for intellectual property rights in general and patents in particular have been matters of controversy since the sixteenth century. As growth in advanced economies has seemingly become more dependent on technological change, the stakes in intellectual property rights have grown. Software and biotechnology, both relatively new areas to come under the patent umbrella, have brought the debate to a fevered pitch in recent years.

The focus on high-tech industries has been especially bright over the last couple of decades. The 1980s saw a flurry of legislative changes, including two that made it easier to obtain patents for publicly funded research.

Today, we still wrestle with the aftermath of several legislative changes and legal precedents. Those who believe that patents indeed provide significant incentives for innovation are generally pleased with recent changes in patent protection, although most still acknowledge the need for more systematic reform of the system. But skeptics worry about several problems, including the strategic use of patents to inhibit innovation.

This collection of essays provides a state-of-the-art analysis of intellectual property rights issues in two frontier industries, software and biotechnology. It is the result of an AEI-Brookings Joint Center conference held on April 30, 2004.

The authors examine a number of fundamental intellectual property issues. These include the general impact of patents on innovation, the measured effects of software patents, the design of optimal software patents, the old patent problems that new technologies have raised afresh, the use of an open source model in biomedical research, and the research conditions that often dictate how intellectual property is dealt with in an industry. After evaluating a number of features of the current system of intellectual property, the authors make some recommendations for reform and suggest areas for future research.

Like all Joint Center publications, this volume can be freely downloaded at www.aei-brookings.org. We encourage educators to distribute these materials to their students.

ROBERT W. HAHN, Executive Director
ROBERT E. LITAN, Director
AEI-Brookings Joint Center for Regulatory Studies

1

Introduction

Robert W. Hahn

Despite decades of research and debate, key questions about the institutional framework protecting intellectual property (IP) have yet to be answered satisfactorily. And the appearance of exciting new technologies in recent years has made the questions all the more urgent. Accordingly, in the spring of 2004 the Joint Center brought together leading scholars to address the protection of intellectual property rights in two frontier industries, software and biotechnology. Specifically, the center asked the specialists to focus on the issue of how intellectual property protection can best be designed to spur innovation without inhibiting follow-on research or denying the public access to the fruits of technological change.

This volume contains their responses. Before reviewing their conclusions, I offer some perspective on the path that intellectual property rights have taken with respect to high-technology innovation. The 1980s and 1990s saw a series of precedent-setting court decisions that dramatically altered the way the law protects property rights in both software and biotechnology.

Pivotal Cases for Software IP Protection

In the 1970s, when software emerged as a product distinct from hardware, the law categorized computer programs as mathematical algorithms. As such, software could not be patented.[1] The Supreme Court confirmed this

I would like to thank Iain Cockburn, Wes Cohen, and Arti Rai for helpful suggestions and comments in drafting this chapter.

interpretation in 1972, when it struck down a patent granted on a new and faster process for converting decimal numbers to binary numbers.[2] A handful of patents awarded later in the 1970s could be classified as software patents today. But, by and large, the 1972 ruling remained unchallenged for the next decade.[3] The common view was that software was best protected by copyright. Accordingly, copyright law formally expanded in 1980 to include software.[4]

In 1981, another Supreme Court ruling dramatically changed IP protection for software.[5] While it did not fully establish the software patenting standards in place today, the *Diamond v. Diehr* decision set the stage for later precedent-setting decisions that extended protection to software. Diehr had developed software for "molding raw, uncured synthetic rubber into cured precision products."[6] The court found this patent valid, reasoning "a claim drawn to subject matter otherwise statutory does not become nonstatutory because a computer is involved."[7] Justice Rehnquist, who wrote for the majority, noted that "the claims must be considered as a whole."[8]

The *Diamond v. Diehr* ruling established that algorithms in a patentee's software were not protected as abstract ideas but in their application in a physical process, such as rubber curing.[9] Software in isolation remained nonpatentable, but creative patent attorneys were now able to wrap software innovations into patents for tangible processes or products.

A year later, another important policy change occurred, with applications not just for software but for all patentable technologies. Prior to that point, those disputing patents could shop for a sympathetic forum among different court circuits. But, with the establishment of the Court of Appeals for the Federal Circuit (CAFC) with overriding jurisdiction, the percentage of appeals found in favor of the patent holder increased by about 50 percent.[10]

A decade later, the importance of the CAFC for the software industry became apparent. The court's *In re Alappat* (1994) decision reversed a U.S. Patent and Trademark Office (USPTO) ruling invalidating a patent for "a means for creating a smooth waveform display in a digital oscilloscope."[11] The USPTO had partly based its decision on the finding that, even though the invention was for use in an oscilloscope (a physical machine), the doctrine of equivalents[12] would protect the use of the same methods on a "general purpose digital computer."[13] Building on *Diehr*, the CAFC rejected this reasoning, instead arguing that "such programming creates a new machine, because a general purpose computer in effect becomes a special purpose computer once it is programmed to perform particular functions pursuant to instructions from program software."[14] *In re Alappat* thus solidified the statutory standing of software patents.

While patents became progressively easier to obtain for software throughout the 1980s and early 1990s, copyright protection was substantially weakened. Early court rulings had favored copyright holders. In 1983, for example, *Apple Computer, Inc. v. Franklin Computer Corp.* protected Apple's exact code and limited what follow-on firms could do without a license.[15] Then, in the mid-1980s, the so-called look-and-feel cases broadened copyright protection to include the organization, interfaces, and structure of a program as well.[16]

One of these cases, *Lotus Development Corp. v. Borland International, Inc.*, made it to the Court of Appeals and then the Supreme Court, where copyright holders hit a brick wall.[17] The Court of Appeals reversed the look-and-feel protection, arguing that follow-on developers had a right to emulate and build on a pioneer's code and methods. The Supreme Court agreed, albeit in a split decision. Given that software is typically malleable, with many different ways of coding the same functions, losing look-and-feel protection in many ways amounted to losing copyright altogether.[18]

Shortly thereafter, the CAFC issued another landmark software patent ruling that eliminated the "business method exception."[19] The *State Street Bank v. Signature Financial Group* decision (1998) reversed a district court ruling invalidating Signature's patent on a "data processing system" for use in its business administering mutual funds.[20] The district court argued that Signature's patent was not valid because "abstract ideas" and "business methods" were not patentable subjects.[21] Drawing on *Diamond v. Diehr* and *Alappat*, the CAFC rejected this nonstatutory claim[22] and went so far as to hold the "business method exception"[23] itself invalid.

State Street proved to be the decisive slip down the proverbial slope: business method, Internet, and other software patent applications have since surged.[24] While many developers still register for copyright protection, it provides little protection except in cases of piracy. Trade secrets, contract restrictions, and patents are the protections of choice for software today.

Turning Points for Biotech IP Policy

The Bayh-Dole Act and Stevenson-Wydler Act both passed in 1980.[25] A primary objective of each was to encourage the development and commercialization of research efforts at nonprofit institutions.[26] In particular, Bayh-Dole allowed universities, where a great deal of biotech research occurs, to retain title to patents resulting from federally funded research and development (R & D) without explicit approval of the agencies underwriting the projects. Because federal funding accounts for around 60 percent of the financial support for the majority of university projects, Bayh-Dole greatly increased the patentability of university research.[27] The Stevenson-Wydler Act made analogous changes in patent policy for research conducted at national laboratories.[28]

In 1980, the Supreme Court also ruled in *Diamond v. Chakrabarty*,[29] striking down the longstanding ban against patenting life forms by confirming a patent on a genetically modified microorganism. The key lay in the modification: The court interpreted the *altered* microorganism as qualifying for a patent because it could be included in "anything under the sun that is man made."[30] Within two years of that decision, the first commercial product made with recombinant DNA techniques—human insulin—was introduced.[31] The USPTO has since granted patents on a multitude of biological material and biotechnology final products.

The CAFC's 1995 *In Re Deuel* opinion extended biotech's reach by making it harder to reject a patent as obvious. The court held that if the precise structure of a human gene sequence is not predictable from prior art, it is not obvious for patenting purposes. Scholars point to this case as crucial in establishing today's low nonobviousness threshold for biotech patents.

Later in the 1990s, the thrust of the biotechnology protection debate shifted from whether innovations were patentable and toward the scope and required level of disclosure in patents that were granted. For example, in 1997, the CAFC narrowed biotech patent scope to match the low nonobviousness standard set by *Deuel*. In *Regents of the University of California v. Eli Lilly & Co*, the Federal Circuit ruled that merely describing a method for isolating a gene or other sequence of DNA was insufficient to establish patent validity; the patent must disclose the full sequence.[32] The resulting patent then covers the exact gene sequence described, along with close structural equivalents.

The 2002 CAFC decision *Madey v. Duke University* centers on a patent issue especially close to the hearts of academic biotech scholars: the research exemption.[33] Unauthorized use of intellectual property has always been illegal. But the "research exemption" was viewed as allowing liberal use for scholarly pursuits and therefore thought to apply to all university research. *Madey* effectively precludes the unlicensed use of IP in any university research, arguing that universities are, in effect, commercial entities that use R & D to compete for funding and prestige. While *Madey* may not eliminate the informal use of the research exemption by individual professors, the ruling is likely to lead university administrators to play a more aggressive role in patent protection.

As in the case of software, laws governing protection of biotech IP have inched their way from complete exclusion from patenting to general acceptance.[34] Also like software, today's biotech debates now center on how patenting should occur. In particular, what are the long-term implications of *Madey*? And, do *Deuel* and *Eli Lilly* define the proper combination of standards for obviousness and scope?

The Policy Debate

Chapter 2, by Robert Hahn, summarizes the economics literature on intellectual property. It reviews the key arguments supporting patents (and copyrights) as spurs to innovation as well as some relatively recent theory suggesting patents can hinder sequential innovation and pose barriers to entry. It also surveys the empirical research on intellectual property protection, which (like the theoretical literature) offers few conclusive results.

Chapter 3, by Stuart Graham and David Mowery, reviews the more prominent controversies in software patenting. In particular, software patent critics have pointed to the patents' poor quality, the stifling effect they can have for follow-on innovations, and their potential for reducing R & D spending. After outlining the difficulties in defining software patents, Graham and Mowery present data on trends in packaged software patenting that highlight the lack of evidence in support of the criticisms. However, the authors are careful to note that empirical support for the benefits of software patents is sparse as well. In the end, they conclude, "Little evidence suggests that increased patenting has been associated with higher levels of innovation in the U.S. software industry, and equally little evidence suggests that increased patenting has proven harmful to innovation in this important sector of the 'post-industrial' economy."

Chapter 4, by Dan Burk and Mark Lemley, analyzes the tensions implicit in the design of software patent policy. Recognizing both the value of patenting for software and the problems with its current application, the authors argue that the courts have gotten software patent rules entirely backward. Court decisions have led to a low patent disclosure standard coupled with a high bar for nonobviousness,[35] which have in turn led to a relatively small number of valid software patents with relatively broad scope. Burk and Lemley conclude that the industry would be better served by detailed patent disclosure and a relatively low bar for nonobviousness—thus a greater number of software patents with narrower scope. The authors then explain why the courts are a better place to fix the rules than Congress or the Patent Office.

In Chapter 5, Iain Cockburn analyzes the patent policy issues that arise from the new field of "bioinformatics." Bioinformatics is biological research conducted using computers. For example, to isolate gene sequences, researchers write search programs that cull through newly created gene databases. This kind of research combines the patent policy problems of both software and biotech, namely, difficulties in searching for prior art, along with inconsistent standards across patents. Patent filers can exploit the differences in standards for disclosure, nonobviousness, and scope across the two fields, describing an invention as either software or biotech to gain the desired standards.

Some observers argue that bioinformatics is about discovery, not invention, and hence should not be eligible for patents at all. But this objection is largely moot, since patents are already being granted in the field. Critics also assert that innovations in bioinformatics are typically sequential, so early patents can hinder later innovation or form barriers to market entry. Open biology research projects, modeled after open source software development, present an important check on the overextension of patent rights.

In Chapter 6, Arti Rai focuses on so-called open biology research, patterned after the open source software development model in which multiple programmers contribute to the software code and make that code available to all users of the resulting program. This contrasts with the traditional software development model. There, users obtain programs in a form that can be read only by computers, and thus the innovations embodied in the software are protected by secrecy.

Biomedical researchers have begun experimenting with open models of research, where data, tools and intermediate results are shared openly with the research community. Thus far, the open model's biggest proponents are drawn from federally funded projects. But, in biomedicine as with software, the open model represents a dramatic departure from the research norm of secrecy and the preference for single lab projects. The pros and cons of open source models are still being debated in the software industry. And, as Rai describes them, the implications of an open research model in biomedicine are even murkier. She concludes that the open model shows some promise for biotechnology research, but whether that promise is fulfilled is an open question.

Chapter 7, by Wesley Cohen, concludes our exploration of high technology IP protection. Cohen suggests that before going much further down the open model road in biotechnology research, practitioners examine the conditions that make open source research workable for specific sorts of software. Where has open source software emerged? Do similar environments and motivations exist for biotech? And, most important, what are the implications of the open model for society's welfare?

While Cohen focuses on biotechnology research, the questions he raises are broadly applicable. How research is conducted affects a whole host of issues ranging from researcher motivations, to the extent of technology diffusion, to the overall level of innovation.

New technologies with commercial potential inevitably raise unique questions about the appropriate degree of intellectual property protection and the appropriate methods for getting from here to there. But, as these essays on aspects of IP protection in software and biotech suggest, there is some common ground. And, investing now in designing the right legal structure for today's technologies will almost certainly pay dividends in the form of a faster, more-sophisticated resolution of IP problems raised by tomorrow's innovations.

Notes

1. The Patent Act of 1952 defines the following as patentable inventions: "any new and useful process, machine, manufacture, or composition of matter, or any new and useful improvement thereof." The courts have long held that mathematical formulae, algorithms, and laws of nature are nonstatutory under the Patent Act. 35 U.S.C. §101. See also *Diamond v. Diehr*, 450 U.S. 175, 185 (1981).

2. *Gottschalk v. Benson*, 409 U.S. 63, 65 (1972).

3. Martin Campbell-Kelly, "Not All Bad: A Historical Perspective on Software Patents," *Michigan Telecommunications and Technology Law Review* (forthcoming); Martin Campbell-Kelly, *From Airline Reservations to Sonic the Hedgehog* (Cambridge, Mass.: MIT Press, 2003); Stuart J. H. Graham and David C. Mowery, "Software Patents: Good News or Bad News?" (chapter 3 in this volume).

4. Adopting the National Commission on New Technological Uses of Copyrighted Works (CONTU) recommendations in its report of 1979, the Copyright Act of 1980 added "computer programs" to the list of copyrightable works.

5. *Diamond v. Diehr*, 450 U.S. 175, 185 (1981).

6. Ibid., 175.

7. Ibid., 181.

8. Ibid., 189. The decision was by a narrow majority, 5–4.

9. Ibid., 192.

10. Adam B. Jaffe, Manuel Trajtenberg, and Michael S. Fogarty, "The Meaning of Patent Citations: Report on the NBER/Case-Western Reserve Survey of Patentees" (working paper no. 7631 NBER, Cambridge, Mass., 2000). See also Glynn Lunney, "Patents, the Federal Circuit, and the Supreme Court: A Quiet Revolution," *Supreme Court Economic Review* 11 (2003): 1–80.

11. *In re Alappat*, 33 F.3d 1526, 1537 (1994).

12. The doctrine of equivalents is the standard for judging the extent of the protection under §112 of the patent code, which states that "such claims shall be considered to cover the corresponding structure, material, or acts described in the specification and equivalents thereof." 35 U.S.C. §112, 6.

13. See note 11, 1545.

14. Ibid.

15. *Apple Computer, Inc. v. Franklin Computer Corp.*, 714 F.2d 1240 (3d Cir. 1983).

16. *Whelan Associates v. Jaslow Dental Labor.*, 609 F. Supp. 1307 (E.D. Pa. 1985); *Computer Assoc. Int'l, Inc. v. Altai, Inc.*, 893 F.2d 26 (1990).

17. *Lotus Development Corp. v. Borland Int'l, Inc.*, 49 F.3d 807 (1st Cir. 1995), *Lotus Dev. Corp. v. Borland Int'l, Inc.*, 116 S. Ct. 804 (1st Circuit decision affirmed without opinion by an equally divided Court); 64 U.S.L.W. 3592 (1996).

18. But not entirely, however. Even today, copyright is viewed as the best way to protect software from piracy (exact duplication).

19. The "business method exception" was a judicial standard for patentability that prevented patents for "methods of doing business." *Hotel Security Checking Co. v. Lorraine Co.*, 160 F. 467 (2d Cir. 1908).

20. *State Street Bank & Trust Co. v. Signature Financial Group Inc.*, 149 F.3d 1368, 1370 (1998).

21. Ibid., 1375.

22. Ibid., 1374.

23. Ibid., 1377.

24. See Josh Lerner, "Where Does *State Street* Lead? A First Look at Financial Patents, 1971–2000," *Journal of Finance* 62 no. 2 (April 2002).

25. Descriptions available at http://www.cogr.edu/bayh-dole.htm and http://www.nttc.edu/aftte/stev_wyd.html. These acts were followed by several more federal laws intended to strengthen the commercial development of nonprofit research, such as the National Technology Transfer and Advancement Act of 1995 and the Technology Transfer Commercialization Act of 2000.

26. Robert Mazzoleni and Richard R. Nelson, "The Benefits and Costs of Strong Patent Protection: A Contribution to the Current Debate," *Research Policy* 27 (April 1998): 273–84. Note that while this paper discusses the theories supporting strong intellectual property rights, the authors argue for a limited use of patents because the associated monopoly power may hinder rather than stimulate technological progress.

27. Jaffe et al., see note 10, 5.

28. The act states that the federal government should strive to transfer federally owned or sponsored technology to state and local governments and to the private sector. In particular, national labs are allowed to partner with the private sector through patent licensing.

29. *Diamond v. Chakrabarty*, 447 U.S. 303, 65 L. Ed. 2d 144, 100 S. Ct. 2204, 1980 U.S. LEXIS 112, 206 U.S.P.Q. (BNA) 193 (1980). The case was decided on a 5–4 vote.

30. Ibid.

31. Stephen A. Merrill, Richard C. Levin, and Mark B. Myers, eds., *A Patent System for the 21st Century* (Committee on Intellectual Property Rights in the Knowledge-Based Economy, Board on Science, Technology, and Economic Policy, Policy and Global Affairs, National Research Council of the National Academies, Washington, D.C., 2004).

32. *Regents of the Univ. of Cal. v. Eli Lilly and Co.*, 119 F.3d 1559, 1997 U.S. App. LEXIS 18221, 43 U.S.P.Q.2d (BNA) 1398 (Fed Cir. 1997).

33. *Madey v. Duke University*, 307 F.3d 1351, 2002 U.S. App. LEXIS 20823, 64 U.S.P.Q.2d (BNA) 1737 (Fed. Cir. 2002).

34. See, for example, Justine Pila, "Bound Futures: Patent Law and Modern Biotechnology," *Boston University Journal of Science and Technology Law* 9 (Summer 2003): 326–78.

35. In order to receive a patent, an invention must not be trivial. That is, it must not be obvious to someone with average skills in the field at hand. A high bar for nonobviousness means that the invention must represent a dramatic improvement over state of the art to receive a patent.

2

An Overview of the Economics of Intellectual Property Protection

Robert W. Hahn

The premise behind government protection of intellectual property (IP) is that well-defined rights provide incentives for creativity. By granting a limited monopoly—limited in both time and scope—a patent allows an inventor to capture a better return on successful research, thereby giving the person the incentive to invest in research with uncertain payoffs in the first place. Or so the classic theory goes.

As anyone familiar with the IP literature knows, though, proving that incentive A leads to invention B is another matter entirely. With a few notable exceptions (pharmaceuticals, for one), economists have been unable to show a clear causal link between increased patent rights and increased innovation. This is an especially crucial link when talking about new technologies, where IP policy is still in the making and therefore can be altered more easily. Added to the mix is an increased dependence on technological change among developed economies. Put simply, the stakes in intellectual property rights have grown dramatically.

In this chapter, I review the economic theory literature on intellectual property rights (IPRs) and the empirical literature that tests those theories. Since much of the explanation for where we are today in software and biotech intellectual property protection is due to the path we have taken, this review is an important step. However, the IP literature is vast and the

I would like to thank Linda Cohen, David Evans, Anne Layne-Farrar, Josh Lerner, Peter Passell, and Scott Wallsten for helpful comments and Sasha Gentling and Chris Nosko for research assistance.

IP court cases extensive. By necessity, this review is selective. Nonetheless, I cover the key issues required to frame an informed debate about IPRs in high-tech industries.

I begin with an overview of the theoretical literature on the role IPRs play in the economy. Theory can be broken into two rough categories. In general, classical theory supports a positive view: that patents, while exacting a price from society, provide incentives to innovate. Other theories along similar themes note that IPRs facilitate information dissemination and the commercial development of ideas. A second strain of the theoretical literature largely agrees with this positive view of IPRs, but notes some exceptions to the rules. In particular, when innovation in an industry is sequential and cumulative, patents can build up quickly to form "thickets" that block subsequent invention. This may be the case both in the software and biotech industries.

So theory tells us that IPRs can do some good (for example, by increasing commercialization) but can also result in innovation-blocking IPRs, especially in today's high-tech industries. Given the "on-the-one-hand" flavor of the theory, the next obvious question is whether the empirical literature helps us distinguish between the conflicting set of possibilities. Unfortunately, much of the empirical research, next reviewed, is just as unclear as the theory. While researchers have reached a consensus in a couple of areas, such as the evidence that strong intellectual property rights assist in the transfer of technology from research institutions, most real-world IP studies raise as many questions as they answer. Certainly, the importance of patent thickets in either software or biotech is still hotly debated.

Measurement issues, including even how to define *innovation*, have troubled the IP literature from the start. What constitutes an innovation may seem obvious in the abstract, but it is difficult to pin down empirically. Several measures of innovation have been used, all of them imperfect. Most commonly, research and development expenditures (R & D) are used as a proxy. The higher the effort expended on R & D, so the reasoning goes, the more innovation will occur. Of course, dollars spent on R & D may not accurately measure research effort. Research staff efficiency is bound to differ across firms, as is their accounting treatment of R & D spending. For instance, tax incentives can induce some companies to categorize informal technological tasks as formal R & D.[1] Firms with identical measured R & D *expenditures* can therefore have dramatically different actual R & D *efforts.* Software R & D is particularly hard to measure, as it is difficult to draw the line between genuine R & D and everyday product development.

While these observations do not bring us closer to answering the basic questions regarding the impact of strengthening intellectual property rights regimes, they do highlight a point that policymakers would be wise to keep in mind: Policy should not rest on any one research effort. The literature is far too complicated for that. The final section offers some conclusions from this complicated literature, as well as some observations about the current state of debate and some policy recommendations.

A Review of IPR Theory

I make no attempt to cover all the theoretical literature. Instead, my goal is to present the key arguments, both for and against the need for strong IPRs, especially as they relate to high-tech industries.

Some Classical Theory: Information Property Rights Increase Innovation. Four related and overlapping arguments support strong IPRs, patents in particular:

1. Patents and copyright provide incentives to innovate because they enable innovators to exclude competition, thereby increasing the expected returns on inventions.

2. Patents provide incentives to turn innovations into commercial products by making it possible to prevent imitation and to sell rights to developers.

3. Patents enhance social welfare by facilitating contracts among inventors and others.

4. Patents enhance social welfare by reducing innovators' incentives to hide information.

The first argument is perhaps the most familiar. The intangible nature of intellectual property sets it apart from physical property. Once exposed, intellectual property often can be easily copied or imitated. Even though the inventor typically bears the costs of creation, it can be difficult for him or her to capture its value. And knowing the creation can easily be appropriated, the inventor's incentive to invent is diminished. Thus, without some system for protecting intellectual property, the economy will underinvest in invention.[2]

In his seminal book, Nordhaus observes that, by preventing others from using an invention for a specified time, patents effectively confer limited monopoly power.[3] Because the inventor can charge monopoly prices for a successful invention (either by selling commercial versions of the invention or by charging royalties for licenses to other producers), he has incentive to invent.[4] Patents therefore partially correct a market failure by offsetting incentives to underinvest. The solution is not complete, though, since the incentives to invent reduce the dissemination of the technology below its optimal level.[5] This is the classic patent trade-off: short-lived monopoly power that reduces output below the socially optimal level in exchange for increased incentives to innovate.

Copyright is based on a similar line of reasoning.[6] An author (of a book or software) must create a work before knowing what the demand for the work will be. Once created, it can be copied easily, making it difficult to earn back the cost of creation. Copyright protects the expression of ideas in the work, preventing rivals from copying, enabling the original creator to recoup his investment and be compensated for the risk of failure, thus providing incentive to create in the first place. Note that copyright, unlike patents, does not protect the idea underlying the creation, just the expression (such as the exact wording and verbatim source code).

The second argument in support of IPRs rests on their role in encouraging commercialization. This is particularly true for patents. As economists recognize, "Many technologically important patents have been issued long before commercial exploitation became possible."[7] Thus, as Kitch notes, patents act like mineral rights claims in which the inventor is the "prospector." The patent defines the boundaries of the claim, giving the patent holder the ability to deter imitations as well as duplicative investments in research in a system that otherwise would depend on trade secrecy.

Equally important, the "prospector" can coordinate subsequent research efforts.[8] Patents allow their holders to signal other firms regarding intended research areas and keep other firms out of their research areas. Patents also allow holders and competitors to contract for synchronized research. Broad patent scope interpretation implies that patent holders have greater incentives to invest in follow-on research for development and commercialization.[9]

Coordinating pioneer and follow-on research requires licensing or contracting of some sort. The third listed argument posits that patents help here as well, facilitating contracts among inventors and producers. Using a model of R & D and licensing in which production techniques can easily be kept secret, Gallini and Winter conclude that "licensing occurs in such a market only if patent protection is available to the licensor."[10] In particular, they develop a two-firm, two-period model with a research phase (the ex ante period) and a production phase (the ex post period). In the ex ante period, a firm with relatively efficient production can offer its competitor a license, sparing the competitor the need to duplicate research and lowering its production costs. The licensor gains through royalty payments as well as by maintaining its dominant market position. If the second firm's costs are close to the first firm's, however, there is no incentive for the sale of a license, and both firms will conduct research in the hope of gaining a competitive advantage. Ex post, the firm with the more successful research (and hence the lower production costs) offers a license to the other firm, with a payoff in the form of royalty payments. "The role of patents in our model is not the traditional role of creating monopolies by *prohibiting* the exploitation of informational spillovers," Gallini and Winter conclude. "Rather, by protecting property rights, patents here *open* the market for trade in technological information."[11]

While the Gallini-Winter model involves patent licensing between two roughly equivalent firms, the Anton and Yao model illustrates how information disclosure operates between an individual inventor and a larger production firm. The two researchers observe that most independent inventors cannot successfully create an organization to commercialize their inventions and therefore must sell their ideas to another party.[12] A potential buyer is rightfully reluctant to pay, sight unseen, for rights to an inventor's creation. But, in the absence of property rights, inventors cannot fully disclose their inventions without risking expropriation by a prospective buyer.

Because of these difficulties, Anton and Yao developed a model in which an independent inventor with weak or nonexistent patent protection can nonetheless capture the value of his invention. An inventor with substantial financial resources can credibly signal the value of that invention by posting a bond that a buyer can keep if the invention is revealed as worthless. This creates an incentive for the buyer to enter into a contract prior to gaining information about the invention. An inventor without adequate resources, however, must disclose the invention to the buyer prior to signing a contract. In this case, the inventor can avoid expropriation by threatening to sell the invention to the buyer's competitor, thereby destroying the potential for monopoly profits. Thus, when intellectual property rights are unavailable, individual inventors must either have substantial resources or deal with competing potential buyers or competing intermediaries such as venture capitalists to capture rents from their inventions. By making information available to potential buyers, patents facilitate inventor-producer negotiations. This line of argument suggests that patents also aid their holders in accessing capital to fund startup companies. That is, rather than seeking out separate producers, inventors can negotiate with financiers to become their own producers.

Merges expands on this point, arguing that some organizational structures for exploiting innovation are feasible only if intellectual property rights are assured.[13] For example, Merges argues that strong IPRs make subcontracting and contract-based "quasi-firms" viable by providing tighter contractual control at a lower cost. Patents provide their holders with a relatively low-cost means of enforcing their rights, which makes patent holders more willing to enter into contracts that require information sharing.[14]

Finally, as noted in the fourth pro-IPR argument, patents can increase social welfare by facilitating information disclosure. As Kitch argues, patents signal research direction and commercialization intentions to competitors. Horstmann, MacDonald, and Slivinski take this argument a step further.[15] They note that patents can convey two types of information: signaling information for potential competitors on the profitability of imitation and direct information, such as which production processes work best. Patents disclose useful information because they "may reveal that some production processes work better than others," information that will be available after patent protection ends.[16] Since trade secrecy is one of the few alternatives to patents, patents provide an additional benefit to society in the form of information disclosure.

Software patents are typically viewed as the exception to this disclosure rule. As Dan Burk and Mark Lemley discuss in chapter 4, recently the courts have set a low threshold for what needs be disclosed in a software patent. Nonetheless, even software patents, with their limited disclosure, improve on the information dissemination lacking with trade secrets.

In the Horstmann et al. model, disclosure is an all-or-nothing proposition: Information embodied in a patent is indivisible. Anton and Yao offer a more nuanced model of patents as signals that allow partial disclosure.[17] After an inventor decides how much information to disclose in a patent, the excluded firm decides whether to challenge the patent's validity in court. Thus, the exclusivity granted by patents is limited not by the information revealed in the patent itself, but by the chance that the patent will subsequently be ruled invalid in court. If a patent is found valid, the inventor is completely protected. If the patent is found invalid, however, competitors are free to use the information provided in the patent. Inventors face a trade-off, because withholding key information can raise the probability that a patent will be found invalid.

All these papers find that patents benefit society. While patents do entail the necessary evil of bestowing limited monopoly power on an inventor, with all the attendant inefficiencies associated with profit-maximizing restrictions in production, they also provide incentives to invest in R & D and to innovate, facilitate the commercialization of inventions, make contracting easier, and improve information disclosure. I turn next to intellectual property theory that holds patents can be harmful to social welfare.

Some Recent Theory: Strong Patents Can Erect Barriers. Much of the literature raising caveats with regard to strong intellectual property rights considers patents in a specific research environment. When innovation is sequential or cumulative, later inventions turn on earlier research. Without coordination associated with information exchange, researchers can duplicate each other's efforts and waste resources. In fields characterized by this kind of learning (software and biotech among them), granting patent rights to "pioneer" inventors can either enable coordinated sequential research (as Kitch argues) or create barriers to follow-on innovations. Here, I discuss four papers that lay out the coordination problems arising when patents are granted early in a sequence of related inventions. The authors suggest licensing strategies and variations in patent rights as a means for reducing the waste, but none argues for eliminating patents altogether.

Scotchmer, a pioneer in this line of theory, observes that "the challenge is to reward early innovators fully for the technological foundation they provide to later innovators, but to reward later innovators adequately for their improvements and new products as well."[18] In Kitch's model, this was not an issue, since the pioneer inventor conducted all follow-on research as well. When multiple parties are involved, however, getting the incentives right is more difficult. The underinvestment problem can be especially acute here, since the full value of the first invention includes not only the direct benefits of the invention but also the boost it provides later researchers, a positive externality in the form of enabling later research, lowering its costs, or speeding its results.

Granting pioneers broad patent rights can overcome the initial incentive problem but can also lead to incentive problems later on, since subsequent developments are more likely to infringe if the first patent is broad. Licensing after follow-on research is completed does not solve this dilemma, because "firms negotiate after all costs have been sunk and patents have been issued."[19]

Scotchmer suggests a priori agreements as the solution: "After the first patent has issued, a potential second innovator could approach the holder of the first patent with an idea for an improvement or new product, and suggest that they share both the costs and the proceeds of research."[20] The relative bargaining strength of these two parties depends on the breadth of the first patent, the degree to which the second invention would infringe on the first, and the production or development capabilities of the second inventor relative to the first. Note that the value of this approach also depends on the ability of the second inventor to disclose the idea to the pioneer without fear of expropriation. In essence, a priori agreements offer a means to return to Kitch's single-firm model, where incentives for sequential invention are not an issue.

Rather than relying on contracting between inventors, Gallini suggests that patent policy—specifically patent length and scope—be used to prevent the wasteful duplicative research.[21] In her simple model, imitation is costly for follow-on researchers but not prohibitively costly. In contrast, Nordhaus assumes that imitating patented goods is so costly that it never occurs.[22] Still other models have assumed that imitation is costless and, therefore, always a threat.[23] In Gallini's intermediate and far more realistic case, a rival decides whether to imitate a patented good, depending on the life of the patent. Longer patents encourage imitation, or "inventing around" the patent, because rivals must wait longer for the technology to become freely available. As a result, increasing patent length may not increase incentives to innovate for the initial researcher, since it implies increased competition from imitators. Under these circumstances, patent authorities should grant broad patents of finite duration both to discourage imitation and to encourage pioneering research.

Similarly, Green and Scotchmer argue that competition from independent follow-on inventors can undermine the profit incentives of pioneers.[24] That is, second inventions that do not infringe on initial inventions compete with them. When the potential loss in profits is severe, it can "stymie the entire line of technology."[25] Green and Scotchmer find that patents should last *longer* when sequential research is not concentrated in one firm. Longer patents are needed to ensure that the first inventor collects some of the profit generated by the second invention, which, after all, was made possible by the initial research.

Shapiro, on the other hand, is more cautious about the benefits of patent rights in sequential-innovation industries. In particular, he argues that "our patent system, while surely a spur to innovation overall, is in danger of imposing an unnecessary drag on innovation by enabling multiple rights owners to 'tax' new products, processes and even business methods."[26] He likens the overlapping patents in some industries to a "patent thicket," a thorny path to be navigated with care. Shapiro also highlights another potential problem in sequential-innovation industries: patent "hold-up." With patent hold-up, new products that inadvertently infringe on patents issued after the new product was designed nonetheless face exorbitant licensing fees. Shapiro contends that patent thickets and hold-up are especially relevant in newer, high technology industries, such as telecommunications, computer software, semiconductors, and biotechnology. Given the nature of research in these industries, even relatively small taxes at each stage can have large cumulative effects.

Rather than touting ex ante agreements, Shapiro suggests that cross-licenses[27] and patent pools,[28] both of which preserve the multiparty nature of the industry, can solve the problems created by the patent thicket. However, in the process of solving property rights allocation problems, cross-licenses and patent pools impose transaction costs. As a result, innovation effort may be lower than the level expected in stand-alone research unencumbered by the need for negotiation. Moreover, the coordination sometimes required for cross-licensing and patent pools may be prohibited by antitrust authorities, who view this kind of activity with suspicion and are leery of jointly set fees of any kind.[29]

This abbreviated tour highlights the fact that patent theory goes only so far. Most questions cannot be answered definitively without examining practice. Are inventors actually able to contract with producers? Do pioneers enter into agreements with sequential researchers before follow-on research occurs? Are cross-licensing and patent pools common in industries characterized by sequential innovation? Do countries with stronger IPRs tend to have greater information sharing and commercial development? In the next section, I consider some of the empirical research relevant to these questions.

The Empirical IPR Literature

Given the nature of the theoretical literature, where changing the assumptions results in dramatically different conclusions and the nature of the research environment plays a pivotal role in determining whether strong intellectual property rights serve society, real-world experience takes on added importance. Here, I examine the empirical research on five questions relevant to policy and the analysis presented in the remainder of this book.[30] First, and most fundamental, do stronger patents lead to increased innovation? Second, do stronger patents increase information disclosure? Third, do stronger patents increase technology transfer? Fourth (and related to the third question), do stronger patents increase commercial development? Fifth, do stronger patents increase economic growth?

Do Strong Patents Spur Innovation? The three papers discussed here cover the range of settings and results.[31] The first examines patent law changes in Japan that would be expected to increase IPRs and thus inno-vation, if the theory outlined earlier holds. The empirical results, how-ever, do not support a link. The second paper, which studies the linkage at the country level instead of the firm level, draws the opposite conclu-sion: Stronger IPRs translate into higher R & D outlays, which leads to stronger innovation. Both papers suggest that variations in institutional factors, such as company and government bureaucracies, are important in interpreting empirical findings. The final paper discussed here empha-sizes the ambiguity in this line of research: It finds both positive and negative effects to patents within the same U.S. industry.

Capitalizing on the opportunity for a natural experiment, Sakakibara and Branstetter analyze evidence from the 1988 patent law reforms in Japan.[32] Prior to 1988, a Japanese patent could include only a single, independent claim for one novel advance.[33] In addition, only specific cases of the product as proven in practice could be patented, as contrasted with the more inclusive ranges for product specifications allowed under the U.S. system. As a result, under the pre-1988 system, Japanese inven-tors needed to apply for multiple patents to protect a single invention. And even when they were successful, the protection left holes. The reforms broadened patent scope to parallel U.S. policy, allowing multiple overlapping claims in a single patent.

In addition to interviewing high-ranking officials at the Japanese Patent Office and IP managers in ten Japanese companies, the authors analyzed several quantitative patent variables. The survey responses indicate that the reforms did, in fact, lead to a significant broadening of patent scope in Japan. And, given the stronger patent scope, the authors expected to see more claims included in each patent filed, fewer patents filed since fewer would be needed to protect an innovation, and improved quality for the inventions patented since stronger IPRs should spur more or better innovation.

The quantitative results, however, were not clear. R & D spending by Japanese firms did increase during the patent reform period. But Sakakibara and Branstetter conclude that little, if any, of this spending is attributable to the reforms, as the upturn began well before the policy changes could have had an impact. On the innovative output side, the authors found that patent applications continued to increase after the reform, but at a decreasing rate, as expected given the nature of the reforms. While the number of claims per patent rose, there was no evidence of higher-quality innovation. For example, patented inventions were not truly broader in scope, in that the new patents did not contain a greater number of International Patent Classification (IPC) subclasses than prereform patents.[34] Nor were postreform patents cited more frequently in other patents, which also would have suggested increased patent quality and more innovation. Overall, the authors conclude that R & D effort and innovative output in Japan was *"unresponsive* to the change in patent scope."[35]

Sakakibara and Branstetter point to an interesting finding that muddles the postulated connection between IPRs and innovation: researchers' organizational structure. Some of the companies the authors interviewed used external patent agents for patent applications, implying that the people conducting the research and those familiar with the patenting process probably had little direct contact.[36] Other companies admitted that their internal incentive structures could inadvertently work to prevent R & D departments from responding to patent law changes. The interviews thus drive home the reality that corporate R & D departments are embedded in larger organizations. Feedback from changes in the patent system to R & D activity is anything but automatic. Japanese organizations may eventually respond to new incentives presented by patent reform, but the change is likely to come slowly.[37] If that is the case, the results that Sakakibara and Branstetter expected to see, but did not, may eventually appear.[38]

In a country-level study, Kanwar and Evenson analyze R & D expenditures in twenty-nine countries from 1981 to 1990.[39] The authors note that patent protection differs across countries in a number of respects, including the range of innovations eligible for patent protection, patent duration, patent enforcement, opportunities for pregrant opposition, and compulsory licensing. For instance, some countries do not allow process patents and others exclude pharmaceuticals, chemicals, and food products.[40] In the authors' data set, patent duration ranges from five to seventeen years. Even countries with equal patent length may start the clock at different points: the application filing date, patent publication date, or patent grant date. The authors capture this variation in an index of IP protection, based on Park and Ginarte.[41] As their measure of innovation, the authors employ R & D investment as a proportion of GNP. They add a number of controls as well, such as savings levels, average education levels, an indicator for political stability, and the real rate of interest on business loans.

On the basis of statistical regression analysis, Kanwar and Evenson conclude that "the strength of intellectual property protection is positively and significantly associated with R & D . . . countries which provided stronger protection tended to have larger proportions of their GDP devoted to R & D activities."[42] In contrast to Sakakibara and Branstetter, then, Kanwar and Evenson find unequivocal support for strong IPRs spurring innovation.

In a single-country single-industry study, Hall and Ziedonis echo both the negative findings of Sakakibara and Branstetter and the positive findings of Kanwar and Evenson.[43] Hall and Ziedonis focus on patenting in the U.S. semiconductor industry from 1979 through 1995. They explore how patent-strengthening policies of the 1980s affected these firms through industry interviews and quantitative analysis of firm-level data on R & D and patenting.[44] The semiconductor industry is particularly interesting because the theoretical literature categorizes technological advances in it as sequential and cumulative. If these theories are valid, patent thickets and hold-up problems should emerge here.

Hall and Ziedonis, indeed, find some evidence of patent hold-up. In particular, they find that large-scale manufacturers appear to be engaged in "patent portfolio races."[45] That is, these firms' aggressive accumulation of patents after the policy changes is not completely explained by other determinants of patenting, such as winning strong legal rights to inventions. Instead, the patents seem to be aimed at providing bargaining chips for negotiations with other firms to obtain access to external technology, what is referred to as *strategic patenting* in the literature. Hall and Ziedonis note, however, that "the semiconductor industry has historically been characterized by broad cross-licenses of patent rights among manufacturers" and this still seems to be the case.[46]

On the other hand, Hall and Ziedonis also find empirical support for the positive effects of stronger patents. They find that firms entering the semiconductor industry after 1982 (that is, entering during the pro-patent era) patent more intensively than other firms in the industry. Specifically, post-1982 design firms appear to be the most patent intensive. Hall and Ziedonis conclude that stronger patent rights were crucial to these firms in securing the intellectual property rights needed to enter niche product markets and attract venture capital funding. Patents, therefore, may have facilitated the observed vertical deintegration between chip design and manufacture; that is, patents may have helped to create the "fab-less" chip design shops.

The contradictory findings in this branch of the literature make it difficult to draw conclusions about the connection between patent strength and innovation. A fundamental disconnection appears between the single-country/single-industry research of Hall and Ziedonis, the single-country/economywide research of Sakakibara and Branstetter, and the multicountry/economy-level research of Kanwar and Evenson. Any number of factors may lie behind the difference in results. Part of the explanation may be that corporations are not the only entities conducting R & D. Or, it may simply be that different industries and different countries respond differently to patent incentives. Perhaps, a narrower study of single industries within Japan would reveal a mix of positive and negative patent effects, just as the U.S. semiconductor study did. It may also be that omitted variables drive R & D in the cross-country study, although that would have to hold for numerous countries to negate Kanwar and Evenson's findings. Finally, it is likely that the measures used to capture country-level R & D are imperfect. Research expenditures are not always reported, or at least fully reported. More problematic, the accuracy in reporting country-level R & D is probably correlated with the attention paid to innovation within a country. This last point implies that patent policy shifts could lead to more complete R & D reporting, which would appear as an increase in R & D, even though underlying innovation remained unchanged. Without further research, it is difficult to know which of these theories (if any) reconcile the divergent conclusions.

Do Patents Increase Information Disclosure? Another fundamental goal of patent policy is to create incentives for information disclosure. Indeed, Merges and Nelson observe that the legal protection encompassed in patents is "premised on an adequate disclosure of the invention" and has been for the entire history of U.S. patent law.[47] This aspect of innovation emphasizes the externalities associated with research and invention, the prospect of social gains on top of the gains to the investors. In other words, past innovation broadens "the shoulders of giants" on which current researchers may "stand."[48] Little empirical work has been done on this subject. I review one paper that explores a recent legal change regarding patent disclosure.

Johnson and Popp focus on patents' "ability to create inspiration for future invention."[49] The American Inventors Protection Act of 2000 changed the rules for patent applications to make the U.S. laws better conform to laws of other countries. Rather than waiting until a patent was granted before publishing it, as had been the U.S. standard, the new law requires U.S. patents to be made public eighteen months after the initial application is filed. Proponents of the law argue that early disclosure makes information about new technologies available sooner and thus helps diffuse knowledge and prevent duplicative research. Moreover, supporters say that the new law will end "submarine" patents—patents where the application process drags on for years, surfacing only after the technology has been widely adopted. Opponents, for their part, argue that early disclosure is particularly harmful to independent inventors, lacking high-powered lawyers, because it removes the secrecy needed to protect against efforts to invent around the patent. This group fears that inventors will choose to keep significant breakthroughs secret rather than applying for a patent. As a result, they claim, the new law actually inhibits disclosure.

To test the hypothesis that the patent policy change would lead to increased disclosure, the authors analyze patent applications from 1976 to 1996. Johnson and Popp measure the significance of an invention by its subsequent citations.[50] They then examine whether patents that take longer from filing to grant are cited more, once they do become public. The authors, in fact, find that patents with longer grant lags are cited more often than the average patent, providing some support to the disclosure opponents who claim the impact of the law would fall disproportionately on "bigger" inventions.[51] As a result of the law, then, relatively more important patents will lose longer secrecy periods as compared to average patents.

Showing that important patents take longer to process, however, does not necessarily imply that earlier disclosure is harmful to society overall. On the other side of the ledger are the benefits that early disclosure can bring through faster diffusion of information. Of course, patent publication is just one venue for sharing information among researchers. Others include scientific publications, research conferences, and personal contact. If patent publications are a key disclosure mechanism, then the rates of citation diffusion and decay for patents with short grant lags should be the same as those with longer grant lags. If, on the other hand, diffusion begins before publication with researchers sharing information, then patents with longer grant lags should have shorter postpublication citation diffusion periods.[52] Johnson and Popp reject the hypothesis that the rates of diffusion are equal. Instead, they find that the citation diffusion period is longer and the rate of decay is slower for patents that take relatively longer to go from application to grant.

Taken as a whole, the authors conclude that information diffusion does indeed begin with patent publication. As a result, they argue that early disclosure is beneficial to the research community in general and should increase the pace of innovation, although it may harm some inventors. This finding underscores the need to alter the current standard for software patent disclosure, which unlike other fields with patent protection has become less and less detailed over time.

Do Patents Increase Technology Transfer? Technology transfer and the diffusion of technical knowledge are often cited as major benefits from innovation. This is related to, but distinct from, the notion of information disclosure. Technology transfer concerns one particular type of information disclosure: the transfer of technical details from an inventor to a commercial developer. A typical goal of an intellectual property rights system is to increase this kind of transfer. Theory suggests that patents can speed technology transfer. What does the evidence show?

I review three papers relevant to this issue. The first two consider technological transfer from university researchers to private industry, examining both the extent and quality of patenting changes in the wake of policy reform. The evidence is clear that technology transfers did increase after patents were made more readily available to universities, although the quality of patented innovations appears to have decreased. The third paper focuses on technology transfer from government-funded research at national laboratories to for-profit companies. It, too, finds that policy changes during the 1980s in the United States led to increased technology transfer from public research facilities to private businesses.

The Bayh-Dole Act of 1980 (the Patent and Trademark Laws Amendment) allowed universities and other nonprofit organizations to retain title to patents resulting from federally funded R & D without needing an explicit waiver from the government agency funding the project. Because federal funding accounted for around 70 percent of the financial support for the majority of university projects at the time, the Bayh-Dole Act greatly increased the patentability of university research.[53] Henderson, Jaffe, and Trajtenberg explore the effect of this policy change on university research and patenting.[54] This is particularly relevant for biotech research, much of which is federally funded and occurs at universities.

Henderson et al. find that university patenting "exploded" in the period after Bayh-Dole.[55] In 1965, twenty-eight U.S. universities received just ninety-six patents. In contrast, in 1992, 150 U.S. universities received nearly 1,500 patents, an increase of over 1,500 percent for a period when total U.S. patenting rose by less than 50 percent. The authors determine that the dramatic rise reflects a significant increase in universities' "propensity to patent." In other words, universities that had never applied for patents began to do so and universities that had always patented began to do so more intensely. Concurrent with the rise in patenting, Henderson et al. find a decline in university patent quality, as measured by patent citations.[56]

While assigning cause and effect is difficult, Henderson et al. conclude that the Bayh-Dole Act was a "success" in raising university incentives to patent and license technology. The citation data, however, indicate that the law had no effect on universities' underlying generation of commercially relevant research. As the authors explain, the lack of citations is not necessarily problematic, although

- Some of these uncited patents are licensed and commercially valuable. Before the Bayh-Dole Act they would probably not have been either patented or licensed, and the invention underlying them would have been unlikely to generate commercial benefits. Thus, the increase in university patenting probably reflects an increased rate of technology transfer to the private sector, and this has probably increased the social rate of return to university research.[57]

- Moreover, the authors note that it is unclear whether society would benefit were universities to shift their efforts toward more

commercially oriented research. Universities are an important
source of basic research. The point of the Bayh-Dole Act was to
move more university research results to the private sector, not to
change the nature of university research.

The conclusions reached by Jensen and Thursby support the view
that patents increase the transfer of technology in university research.[58]
The authors present survey results that highlight the embryonic nature of
university inventions: Most "are little more than a 'proof of concept.'"[59]
They find that universities typically license inventions so early in development that no one knows whether they can be successfully commer-
cialized. These inventions require substantial development effort, often
involving the original inventor as well as the licensee.

Jaffe and Lerner examine technology transfer at the federally funded
national laboratories.[60] In particular, the authors study how research at
labs owned by the U.S. Department of Energy responded to the 1980
Stevenson-Wydler Act (formally known as the Technology Innovation Act
of 1980).[61] The act, among other things, allowed national labs to form
partnerships with private industry through patent licensing.

One interesting finding that emerges from the Jaffe-Lerner study is
that politics play a prominent role in technology transfer. Those facilities
with contractor turnover, and thus less pressure from old-line parties
resistant to exclusive licensing, had relatively more success in commercializing their research. Moreover, the type of contractor running the
facility had an impact on patent licensing. Some of the contractors were
universities, where patenting and licensing practices were more clearly
established; this had a positive impact on licensing efforts. These findings
(that bureaucratic factors influence technology transfer) echo the findings
in Sakakibara and Branstetter's study of corporate research in Japan and
suggest a complicated relationship between the organizational structure
of research and both innovation and technology transfer.[62]

Unlike many other avenues of IPR research, the available evidence
here strongly favors the view that patents facilitate technology transfer.
The studies reviewed conclude that stronger patenting rights have led to
increased technology sharing among universities, national laboratories,
and private firms. This was precisely the aim of several of the patent

reforms instituted in the 1980s, namely, the Bayh-Dole and Stevenson-Wydler Acts. Thus, at least in this one instance, policy goals and the resulting legislation led to desired behavior changes among federally funded researchers.

Do Patents Increase Commercial Development? As Jaffe and Lerner observe, "The act of technology transfer . . . only begins the process of incorporating this technology into commercial innovation."[63] The next step is industry development of an invention into a viable product. The three papers I review in this section examine whether patents play a positive role in transforming an invention into a usable product. The first examines historical examples and concludes that broad patent rights hinder the licensing necessary for commercial development. The second finds that patents can facilitate the financial investments that make commercialization possible. The final paper concludes that strong IPRs can facilitate licensing trade secrets in addition to the patented technology itself.

Merges and Nelson argue that the contribution patents make to commercializing an invention hinges on the patent's scope and the nature of the technology.[64] The authors present case study evidence on several industries within the United States: electrical lighting, automobiles, airplanes, semiconductors and computers, chemicals, and radios. They find that broad patent rights hindered extensive development of these cumulative technologies. For example, they argue that Seldon, a pioneer in automobiles who patented an early, pivotal engine design, never "used the patent to orchestrate the efficient improvement of automobile technology; there was no policy of 'developing the prospect.'"[65] In contrast, the initial transistor patents that AT&T held were broadly licensed at low royalty rates. Merges and Nelson hold, however, that the ensuing commercialization was driven by the antitrust consent decree that prevented AT&T from entering the commercial transistor business. AT&T had every incentive to license the patents because it could not profit by developing its own product.

The authors conclude that, while patents provide important incentives for pioneers, their scope should be carefully delineated. There is no guarantee that patent pools, cross-licensing, or company consolidations will be able to "break an industry impasse" and lead to technology transfer or commercialization.[66] While Merges and Nelson readily admit the path that the examined technologies would have taken under a different patent regime is unknown, they contend that their case study evidence shows inventors granted broad rights were not always successful in coordinating their activities through licensing agreements, while those with more narrowly defined patents were successful in licensing.

Lerner also focuses on patent scope in aiding commercialization, although he asks a different question.[67] He employs data on multiple financing rounds for privately held, venture-backed biotechnology firms to examine the impact of patent scope on firm value, where scope is measured by the number of IPC subclasses into which the U.S. Patent and Trademark Office assigns a patent. Using regression analysis, Lerner found that both the number and scope of patents contribute significantly to a firm's value. In particular, an increase in average patent scope by one standard deviation leads to a 21 percent increase in the firm's valuation.[68] Lerner also finds that the marginal value of broader patent scope is higher when the firm has competitors selling substitute products. When a product is highly differentiated (that is, has few substitutes), the firm producing it receives less value from a relatively broad patent. Given that product competition in biotechnology is immature and alternative means for protecting intellectual property are not very effective, Lerner's findings suggest that patents are important in this industry.

Arora, Fisfori, and Gambardella focus on the exchange of technology among firms.[69] While Lerner concludes that strong patents can translate into higher market values, Arora et al. find that stronger patents lead to more-efficient technology licenses, both for patented and unpatented technology. The authors argue that firms can craft better contracts, ensuring both that licensees pay the contracted fees and that licensors deliver the contracted technology, by exploiting complementarities between patented technology and trade secrets. Transferring tacit know-how is costly and difficult, often requiring individual training. On the licensor's side, there is little to guarantee that the technology recipient will pay after the transfer; after all, it cannot "unlearn" and return what the licensor has taught it. On the licensee's side, there is little to guarantee that the licensor will send its best engineers or transfer all it knows. In light of this well-known conundrum, drafting an enforceable contract is virtually impossible without some additional means to ensure compliance.

That is where patents come in. The licensor can revoke the use of a patent if the licensee fails to pay after receiving the trade-secret portion of the knowledge transfer. The licensee can refuse to pay royalties if the licensor does not transfer adequate know-how. Arora et al. test whether patents facilitate the transfer of trade secrets by examining 144 technology import agreements by Indian firms from 1950 through 1975. Even after controlling for industry characteristics and the size of the licensee, the empirical analysis shows that the provision of intangible technical services is accompanied by the provision of tangible complementary inputs, such as patent licensing and equipment supply. The authors conclude that "better IPR laws in countries which rely upon licensing . . . as a source of technology transfer would enhance the inflow of know-how and make the technology transfer more efficient."[70]

While not as scattered as the empirical research on patents and innovation nor as positive as the research on technology transfer, the papers presented here offer some evidence that patent strength can positively affect commercial development.

Do Patents Increase Economic Development? Some economists have carried the theory that patents can have positive effects on innovation to its logical conclusion by arguing that strong IPRs lead to economic growth. But empirical analyses do not yield clear-cut results. I review three papers that examine this issue: one multicountry study with positive results, one single-country study with somewhat positive results, and one multicountry study with ambiguous results.

Park and Ginarte study data on a cross-section of countries from 1960 to 1990.[71] The authors reason that strong patents encourage research by reducing the risks of imitation and piracy. In turn, R & D affects the technical efficiency of production and leads to increased economic output. To test this hypothesis, Park and Ginarte construct an index of patent protection strength for sixty countries. The index measures five categories of protection: patent coverage, country membership in international patent agreements, provisions for loss of protection, presence of enforcement mechanisms, and patent duration. Coverage, for instance, refers to whether the country allows patents for utility processes, pharmaceuticals, and chemical products. Loss of protection encompasses items such as compulsory licensing or potential patent revocation.

The authors use their index as a variable in a system of regression equations that estimate the effect of a country's patent regime on its economic growth, capital investments, education levels, and R & D expenditures. They find that "intellectual property protection is a significant determinant of physical and R & D capital accumulation, even after controlling for market freedom."[72] This effect translates into increased economic growth, as innovations alter the structure of the production function and result in more output for a given level of inputs. Other regression results suggest that developed countries may drive these results, however: The IPR index had a positive but statistically insignificant impact for developing countries (DCs). This result could reflect the greater proportion of R & D devoted to imitation, which would tend to *decline* as intellectual property rights are strengthened.

Park and Ginarte conclude that policymakers should not limit their focus to intellectual property rights laws. Institutions play an integral part in any IPR regime. Countries pursuing innovative R & D, as contrasted to imitative R & D, are more likely to have the incentives (and therefore the political will) to establish costly institutions for IPR development and enforcement.

Lanjouw uses public data and personal interviews to explore innovative versus imitative research in India's pharmaceuticals industry.[73] The Uruguay Round of the GATT Treaty, among other things, made conferring patent protection on pharmaceuticals a condition of membership in the World Trade Organization. India, which did not provide such protection prior to the treaty, was particularly vocal in opposing it, equating patenting pharmaceuticals to "profiteering from life and death."[74] Proponents argued that product imitation in DCs cost the developed world substantial sums, and that stronger IPRs would also benefit DCs by encouraging foreign investment, technological transfer, and greater domestic R & D.

In 1970, India instituted a number of policies aimed at making the country self-sufficient in medicines. As part of that reform, it substantially weakened intellectual property rights, prohibiting product patents altogether for pharmaceuticals, agrochemicals, and food. The government also instituted price controls for a large portion of the drug market. The reforms had the desired effect: By 1991, domestic firms produced 70 percent of the bulk drugs and 80 percent of the formulations used in the country.[75]

Much of the production, however, was imitative. Indian firms produced drugs still under patent in Europe or the United States for sale in India. When patents expired, Indian producers were some of the first to come to the global market with generic versions. Introducing pharmaceutical patents into this environment would eliminate India's imitative R & D and could also slow the country's entrance into the global market for generics.

However, Lanjouw found that only a small portion of India's production consisted of drugs still under patent. Of the top 500 brands, drugs containing patented substances amounted to only 11 percent of sales. Therefore, introducing patent protection is not likely to affect either drug production or the welfare of most drug consumers within the country. Nor is the patent regime change likely to affect India's balance of payments. As for generic drugs in the global market, the author observes that low manufacturing costs can be decisive in driving sales.[76] Thus, even without first-mover advantages, India retains a key advantage in the form of relatively low labor costs. The country is therefore likely to remain an important supplier of generic drugs despite the imposition of drug product patents that delay manufacture until patents expire.

On the negative side, Lanjouw's research suggests that, despite the policy change to conform to international rules, India may have trouble attracting multinational corporations (MNCs) willing to manufacture drugs covered by patents. First, India's drug price controls are still in place and could interfere with MNCs' global drug pricing strategies. Unless India eliminates its price controls when it introduces drug patents, MNCs would have little profit motive to increase either manufacture or sales within the country. Administrative hurdles are also formidable in India: In practice, the Drugs Controller General requires manufacturers to show not just that a drug is safe and effective (as in the United States) but also that it is needed. These factors suggest that adding patent protection likely will not increase drug technology transfer linked to MNC production in India. Finally, Lanjouw concludes that allowing drug patents would lead to more-innovative R & D within India. She notes that the disease patterns are quite different for DCs than for developed countries. Diseases such as malaria and leprosy are significant problems within India but have largely disappeared in the developed world. Allowing drug patents increases incentives for Indian R & D efforts targeted at regional diseases.

A broader, multicountry study by Branstetter, Fisman, and Foley yields equally ambiguous results on the impact of stronger IPRs on international technology transfer.[77] The authors analyze firm-level data for a number of countries that reformed their patent policies in the 1980s and 1990s. The focus is on U.S.-based multinationals with foreign subsidiaries. They look for evidence of either increased profit taking in the wake of patent reform or increased licensing of new technology.

Branstetter et al. find a bit of both: "The data do not tell a simple story of either pure rent extraction or only an increase in the volume and sophistication of technology being transferred. Rather, the data suggest that both are taking place in the aftermath of patent reform."[78] In particular, the authors find that royalty flows from affiliates to MNCs increase by around 9 percent, indicating that technology transfers from parent to subsidiary are modestly higher after reform.[79] For firms with larger-than-average patent portfolios, however, the increase is a more substantial 26 percent.[80] Similarly, employment, sales, costs, and return on assets for affiliates as a whole do not change much with patent reform, but they do increase substantially for the large patent portfolio group.[81]

These results are consistent with two distinct corporate responses to patent reform. They could signal price increases resulting from greater market power due to patents, or they could signal an increase in the amount of technology supplied to affiliates abroad. To determine which of the competing interpretations is correct, Branstetter et al. extend their analysis. They find that nonresident patent filings increase 35 percent after reform, indicating that at least some technology transfer is occurring.[82] Moreover, the increase in patent filings is sustained, implying that the numbers do not merely reflect a one-time jump in patenting for existing technology. The authors conclude that their "results may be tentatively interpreted as being consistent with an increase in both real flows of technology and greater rent extraction by multinationals."[83]

A complex set of results emerges from the empirical research considering the correlation between patent strength and economic growth. Park and Ginarte find that patent strength, measured at the country level on several dimensions, encourages the accumulation of both physical and R & D capital. Their result holds primarily for developed economies, though; in developing nations, the link is not statistically significant. In studying just one country, Lanjouw argues that introducing patent protection for pharmaceutical drugs would not lead multinationals to increase either their R & D or production investments in India. However, allowing patents in this field, she contends, would shift local Indian research away from imitative efforts toward more innovative research without having any substantial adverse effect on India's ability to compete in the off-patent generic drug market.[84] Branstetter et al. find that increasing patent strength leads to more profit taking on the part of U.S.-based multinationals. But, stronger patents in developing countries also seem to generate greater technology transfers from the U.S. parent company to local affiliates. Taken as a whole, these results indicate that altering patent strength affects a host of factors and leads to some desired and some not-so-desired outcomes. The key for economic development, then, is setting patent policy so that the desired effects outweigh the undesired ones.

The Crucial Role of Data and Measurement. In closing this review of empirical IPR literature, I turn to a study that comments on the dire state of the empirical data used to examine intellectual property rights: Zvi Griliches's 1994 American Economic Association Presidential Address. Griliches focuses on a recurring point in the empirical literature on IPRs: "Our understanding of what is happening in our economy (and in the world economy) is constrained by the extent and quality of the available data."[85] He refers to research on the link between R & D and economic growth, but his comments are more broadly applicable, as will be apparent in the chapter on software patent trends by Graham and Mowery.

Griliches begins his address by outlining the "facts." First, measured productivity growth in the United States slowed sometime in the 1960s. Second, patents per R & D dollar began declining well before the 1960s, probably as early as the 1920s. But most economists did not take note of the change until the 1970s, with its oil-price shocks, stagflation, and rise in the dollar exchange rate. Patents per scientist and per researcher have been declining since the 1920s as well.

How should one interpret this combination of events? Some researchers conclude that the underlying pace of technical change really did decline—that whatever growth was spurred in the late 1930s was interrupted by the Second World War and then exhausted. One possible cause for this malaise is diminishing returns to scientific and technical research. Griliches rejects this view and instead argues that the best we can do is reach a verdict of "not proven."[86]

A number of factors buttress Griliches's conclusion. For one thing, measuring economic productivity is very difficult. In the 1930s, over half of the U.S. economy was engaged in sectors with easily measurable output, such as agriculture, mining, and manufacturing. By the 1980s, those sectors were a much smaller part of our economy. In contrast, recent growth sectors, such as trade, finance, and other services, resist productivity measurement.

Data collection has not kept pace with the changing economy. While the government price series for computer-related products is now "quality adjusted" to reflect technological improvements to the underlying products, many other data series have not received similarly needed overhauls.[87] Pharmaceuticals likely fall in this category because government price series treat generics as separate commodities. As drug patents expire and generics enter the market, the measured price index does not fall, since the brand owners usually choose to maintain their patent-level prices and settle for a smaller market share. As a result, the measured value of shipments declines and so does measured output. In reality, though, output typically expands as average price falls.[88] If generics were included with original branded drugs, a more accurate description of output would be possible.

On the other side of the growth-IPR equation, patents appear to have changed over time, as have R & D reporting procedures. For instance, changes in patenting standards and allowable categories imply that simple patent counts can be misleading. As informal technological activities are reclassified as formal research—a result of tax incentives—reported R & D expenditures increase. As Griliches notes, "Given the presence of so many opposing forces, there is no compelling need to reply on the exhaustion-of-inventive-opportunities hypothesis."[89] While not very satisfying, this is likely the best we can do at present on pinning down the relationship between intellectual property rights, R & D expenditures, and economic productivity.

Conclusions

While not exhaustive, this review of the literature and the law on intellectual property rights covers the salient features necessary for understanding the current debate over IP protection. Some of the research discussed here demonstrates a link between stronger patent rights and social benefits. For instance, the evidence clearly shows that allowing patents for federally funded research at universities and national labs has led to increased technology transfer to industry. Other findings indicate that R & D rises with IPR strength. However, some research lands in the opposite camp. Some historical evidence, for instance, suggests broad patent rights inhibit the commercial development of technologies that are cumulative in nature. Still other results are ambiguous, indicating, for example, that patents appear to be strategically useful to companies but also appear to lower entry barriers and increase competition among niche players. Thus, despite its long history, the literature on intellectual property rights has found few hard conclusions.

Nonetheless, from this less-than-decisive set of findings, a couple of broad themes emerge. First, measuring the actual impact of strong patents on innovation, commercialization, or economic growth is difficult to do well. The available data are inadequate to the task, and while findings based on the numbers are suggestive and provocative, they are seldom conclusive. Consequently, a study's underlying assumptions and methodology take on added importance. As we discovered in reviewing the theoretical literature, assumptions often drive conclusions. Mundane issues like the quality of data sampling can bias findings. Griliches warned against taking data at face value; to understand analytic output, we need to understand its inputs. Fundamentally, a study's results rest on the data and the methods employed in the analysis.

Second, institutional factors, ranging from the structure of research organizations to seemingly tangential laws, appear to play a critical role in how patent policy gets translated into innovation and R & D. As Shleifer notes, "Political economy over the last two centuries, as well as recent empirical research, demonstrate that [public and private] institutions differ tremendously and systematically among countries, and that these differences have significant consequences for economic and political performance.[90] Research that ignores the institutional setting of its subject is bound to fall short in explaining the complex relationships between patents and innovation.

On the basis of this analysis, I offer three modest recommendations.

- *Data collection efforts should receive increased attention.* In particular, more-inclusive measures of R & D and more-accurate measures of output (quality adjusted) should be a high priority for government agencies. More-detailed data on technology licensing should be a high priority for economists. I am sure many other measurement tasks could be added to this list as well. Too often, data collection is relegated to the bottom of the priority list.

- *Follow-up research studies after patent policy changes are implemented should hold a higher priority.* It is important to know the effects of enacted legislation and policy shifts to properly evaluate the need for additional policy changes. When laws are made, they should include data collection and analysis provisions designed to allow careful evaluation of the policy. If we hope to do better in crafting intellectual property rights policy, we must learn from our past successes and failures.

- *Proposed policy changes should draw on the complete literature.* As the preceding review illustrates, the literature is full of contradictory findings. Policy changes based on empirical results should account for all the findings and not rely on any one study. Attempts should be made to reconcile the literature when results are at odds with one another. Narrow reliance on a subset of findings runs the risk of ignoring important caveats that could better guide the policy.

Notes

1. See the discussion in Zvi Griliches, "Productivity, R & D, and the Data Constraint," *American Economic Review* 84, no. 1 (1994): 9.

2. See, e.g., Kenneth Arrow, "Economic Welfare and the Allocation of Resources for Inventions," in *The Rate and Direction of Inventive Activity: Economic and Social Factors*, ed. R. Nelson (Princeton, N.J.: Princeton University Press, 1962), 619.

3. William Nordhaus, *Invention, Growth and Welfare: A Theoretical Treatment of Technological Change* (Cambridge, Mass.: MIT Press, 1969), 70.

4. Edmund Kitch refers to this line of argument as the "reward theory" for patents. "The patent is a reward that enables the inventor to capture the returns from his investment in the invention, returns that would otherwise (absent secrecy) be subject to appropriation by others." Edmund Kitch, "The Nature and Function of the Patent System," *Journal of Law and Economics* 20, no. 2 (1977): 266.

5. The marginal cost of production and dissemination is near zero after invention, implying that optimal allocation is nearly unlimited. By allowing the inventor to raise price above cost, patents limit technology dissemination. See Arrow, "Economic Welfare and the Allocation of Resources for Inventions," 615. Cited in note 2.

6. See, e.g., William M. Landes and Richard A. Posner, "An Economic Analysis of Copyright Law," *Journal of Legal Studies* 18 (1989): 325, 325–33, 344–53.

7. Kitch, "Nature and Function of the Patent System," 267. Cited in note 4.

8. Ibid., 276. Note that Kitch argues for a combination of trade secrets and patents, not for patents eliminating trade secrets; ibid., 275.

9. Ibid., 268, 276.

10. Nancy T. Gallini and Ralph A. Winter, "Licensing in the Theory of Innovation," *RAND Journal of Economics* 16, no. 2 (1985): 238.

11. Ibid. Emphasis in original.

12. James Anton and Dennis Yao, "Expropriation and Inventions: Appropriable Rents in the Absence of Property Rights," *American Economic Review* 84, no. 1 (1994): 190. See also James Anton and Dennis Yao, "The Sale of Ideas: Strategic Disclosure, Property Rights, and Contracting," *Review of Economic Studies* 69, no. 3 (2002): 513–31.

13. Robert Merges, "Expanding Boundaries of the Law: Intellectual Property and the Costs of Commercial Exchange," *Michigan Law Review* 93 (1995): 1570.

14. In principle, all of the rights conveyed by patents could be specified in a contract. However, Merges notes that, in practice, enforcing contracts, especially ones with detailed nonstandard provisions, is difficult. Patents are a standardized set of rights and thus lower contracting costs. Ibid., 1573–74.

15. Ignatius Horstmann, Glenn M. MacDonald, and Alan Slivinski, "Patents As Information Transfer Mechanisms: To Patent or (Maybe) Not to Patent," *Journal of Political Economy* 93, no. 5 (1985): 837–58.

16. Ibid., 849.

17. James Anton and Dennis Yao, "Patents, Invalidity, and the Strategic Transmission of Enabling Information," *Journal of Economics and Management Strategy* 12, no. 2 (Summer 2003): 151–78.

18. Suzanne Scotchmer, "Standing on the Shoulders of Giants: Cumulative Research and the Patent Law," *Journal of Economic Perspectives* 5, no. 1 (Winter 1991): 29–41, 30.

19. Ibid., 35.

20. Ibid., 36.

21. Nancy T. Gallini, "Patent Policy and Costly Imitation," *RAND Journal of Economics* 23, no. 1 (Spring 1992): 52–63.

22. See Nordhaus, 76. Cited in note 3.

23. See, e.g., Richard J. Gilbert and Carl Shapiro, "Optimal Patent Length and Breadth," *Rand Journal of Economics* 21, no. 1 (Spring 1990): 106–12.; and Paul Klemperer, "How Broad Should the Scope of Patent Protection Be?" *RAND Journal of Economics* 21 (Spring 1990): 113–30.

24. Jerry Green and Suzanne Scotchmer, "On the Division of Profit in Sequential Innovation," *RAND Journal of Economics* 26, no. 1 (1995): 20–33

25. Ibid., 20.

26. Carl Shapiro, "Navigating the Patent Thicket: Cross Licenses, Patent Pools, and Standard Setting," in *Innovation Policy and the Economy*, vol. 1, ed. Adam B. Jaffe, Josh Lerner, and Scott Stern (Cambridge, Mass.: MIT Press, 2001).

27. Under a cross-licensing agreement, two firms agree to license all or most of the other's patents. Sometimes, the cross-licensing agreements are automatic, with each party to the agreement receiving a license on each new patent as a matter of course for a specified time into the future. The licensing agreement can involve "balancing payments" that reflect the relative strengths of the patent portfolios. They may specify either up-front fixed payments or running royalties. Ibid., 12.

28. With patent pools, a single entity, such as an industry association or one of the original patent holders, licenses the patents of two or more companies to third parties as a complete package. Thus, patent pools can offer the convenience of "one-stop shopping" for licensees and the benefit of combining patents of little value on an individual basis into a package of significant value for licensors. Ibid., 17.

29. For suggested antitrust authority guidelines on dealing with patent pools, see Josh Lerner and Jean Tirole, "Efficient Patent Pools" (working paper no. 9175, NBER, Cambridge, Mass., September 2002).

30. The focus in this section is on patents. While there are some empirical copyright papers (see, e.g., Stephen Breyer, "The Uneasy Case for Copyright: A Study of Copyrights in Books, Photocopies, and Computer Programs," *Harvard Law Review* 84 [1970]: 281; and Robert M. Hurt and Robert M. Schuchman, "The Economic Rationale of Copyright," *American Economic Review* 56, nos. 1–2 [March 1966]: 421–32), much of the literature on copyrights is either theoretical or speculative. Breyer concludes, and others following him concur, that the cost-benefit calculations

would not support creating a copyright system de novo today, but given that one already exists, they do not justify abolishing the one we have, either. (See Breyer, just cited, and Mark S. Nadel, "Questioning the Economic Justification for (and Thus Constitutionality of) Copyright Law's Prohibition against Unauthorized Copying: §106" (AEI-Brookings, January 2003), available at http://www.aei-brookings.org/publications/index.php?tab=author&authorid=265.

31. There are certainly many more papers on this topic, but the three discussed here cover the various strains of results found in the literature.

32. Mariko Sakakibara and Lee Branstetter, "Do Stronger Patents Induce More Innovation? Evidence from the 1988 Japanese Patent Law Reforms," *RAND Journal of Economics* 32, no. 1 (Spring 2001): 77–100.

33. "As each patent was so thinly defined under the Japanese patent system, some critiques even called it the *sashimi* system, after the Japanese sliced fish delicacy." Ibid., 79.

34. The authors follow Lerner and use the number of International Patent Classification subclass codes as a proxy of true patent scope. See Josh Lerner, "The Importance of Patent Scope: An Empirical Analysis," *RAND Journal of Economics* 25, no. 2 (Summer 1994): 319–33.

35. Sakakibara and Branstetter, "Do Stronger Patents Induce More Innovation? Evidence from the 1988 Japanese Patent Law Reforms," 98. Cited in note 32. Emphasis in original.

36. Ibid.

37. As a historical illustration, Lamoreaux and Sokoloff found that the effects of the U.S. Patent Act of 1836, which established the current system of patent examination, took several years to appear at all and many more years to culminate. See Naomi R. Lamoreaux and Kenneth L. Sokoloff, "Inventive Activity and the Market for Technology in the United States, 1840–1920," (working paper 7107, NBER, Cambridge, Mass., May 1999), 8.

38. Of course, even if this is the case, it will be nearly impossible to ascribe the increases in R & D and patent quality to patent reform that took place years earlier.

39. Sunil Kanwar and Robert E. Evenson, "Does Intellectual Property Protection Spur Technological Change?" *Oxford Economic Papers* 55, no. 2 (2003): 235–64 (previously, Yale University, Economic Growth Center, Center Discussion Paper No. 831, June 2001).

40. Ibid., 10.

41. See Walter G. Park and Juan Carlos Ginarte, "Intellectual Property Rights and Economic Growth," *Contemporary Economic Policy* 15 (July 1997): 51–61. I discuss this paper later in this chapter.

42. Kanwar and Evenson, "Does Intellectual Property Protection Spur Technological Change?" 18. Cited in note 39.

43. Bronwyn H. Hall and Rosemarie Ham Ziedonis, "The Patent Paradox Revisited: Determinants of Patenting in the U.S. Semiconductor Industry, 1979–95," *RAND Journal of Economics* 35, no. 1 (2001): 101–28.

44. In addition to the Bayh-Dole and Stevenson-Wydler acts, which extended patenting rights to government-funded research, the 1980s also saw the creation of a specialized appellate court with jurisdiction over patents, the Court of Appeals for the Federal Circuit (CAFC). I discuss these changes in greater detail later in this chapter. Scholars have interpreted these changes, as well as changes in court decisions, as signaling a new pro-patent era in the legal environment in the United States. Ibid., 105.

45. Ibid., 104.

46. Ibid., 109.

47. Robert Merges and Richard Nelson, "On the Complex Economics of Patent Scope," *Columbia Law Review* 90 (1990): 839, 844–45.

48. Sir Isaac Newton to Robert Hooke, "If I have seen further it is by standing on the shoulders of Giants," http://www.warble.com/jherbert/giants.html (accessed October 28, 2003).

49. Daniel Johnson and David Popp, "Forced Out of the Closet: The Impact of the American Inventors Protection Act on the Timing of Patent Disclosure," *RAND Journal of Economics* 34, no. 1 (Spring 2003): 96–112.

50. Other measures of patent significance include commercial value, as captured by patent renewal data (if a patent is not commercially valuable, its holder will not expend the resources necessary to renew it) and by international protection data (inventors of more-valuable patents are more likely to expend the resources necessary to obtain patent protection in multiple countries). Johnson and Popp are interested less in the commercial value than in the social value of a patent and therefore use patent citations as the measure of patent significance. Ibid., 99.

51. While Johnson and Popp found support for more significant inventions taking longer to process, and thus losing more of the secrecy period than other patents, the authors found that the grant lags for independent inventors were practically identical to those for U.S. businesses. Ibid., 97, note 1.

52. For a graphical depiction of this hypothesis, see ibid., 108, figure 4.

53. A description of the act is available at http://www.cogr.edu/search/Doc Viewer.cfm?DocName=Bremerarticle.htm. Bayh-Dole was followed by the Trademark Clarification Act of 1984 (Public Law 98-620), which expanded university rights further by removing certain restrictions regarding the kinds of inventions that universities could own. See http://www.gnet.org/government/lawlibrary/1801.cfm.

54. Rebecca Henderson, Adam B. Jaffe, and Manuel Trajtenberg, "Universities As a Source of Commercial Technology: A Detailed Analysis of University Patenting, 1965–1988," *Review of Economics and Statistics* 80, no. 1 (February 1988): 119–27.

55. Ibid., 119.

56. They use citation counts to capture patent "importance" and the extent to which citations belong to different patent classes to capture patent "generality." Ibid., 123.

57. Ibid., 126.

58. Richard Jensen and Marie Thursby, "Proofs and Prototypes for Sale: The Tale of University Licensing," *American Economic Review* 91, no. 1 (1998): 240–59.

59. Ibid., 240.

60. Adam Jaffe and Josh Lerner, "Reinventing Public R & D: Patent Policy and the Commercialization of National Laboratory Technologies," *RAND Journal of Economics* 32, no. 1 (2001).

61. A description of the act is available at http://www.reeusda.gov/1700/legis/ techtran.htm. Stevenson-Wydler was followed shortly by another act aimed at technology transfer for federally funded research, the Federal Technology Transfer Act of 1986. The 1986 act authorized the federal laboratories to enter into Cooperative Research and Development Agreements (CRADAs) with universities, nonprofits, and private companies.

62. Jaffe and Lerner add one final caveat to their findings. Licensing activities, while clearly increasing technology transfer, may also distract national lab researchers from their "key missions." Ibid., 194. To address this cost-benefit trade-off question, the authors suggest analyzing the extent to which interactions between labs and firms inform and enhance or detract from other traditional R & D efforts at the national labs. They note, however, that data on this question are difficult to obtain.

63. Ibid., 194.

64. Merges and Nelson, "On the Complex Economics of Patent Scope." Cited in note 47.

65. Ibid., 889. Merges and Nelson point to the bulk chemicals industry as an example of limited patent scope leading to pervasive cross-licensing. Ibid., 898.

66. Ibid., 896.

67. Josh Lerner, "Importance of Patent Scope: An Empirical Analysis." Cited in note 34.

68. Other independent variables are evaluated at their mean. Ibid., 327.

69. Ashish Arora, Andrea Fosfuri, and Alfonso Gambardella, *Markets for Technology* (Cambridge, Mass.: MIT Press, 2001).

70. Ibid., 140.

71. Park and Ginarte, "Intellectual Property Rights and Economic Growth." Cited in note 41.

72. Ibid., 59.

73. Jean Lanjouw, "The Introduction of Pharmaceutical Product Patents in India: Heartless Exploitation of the Poor and Suffering?" (working paper no. 6366, NBER, Cambridge, Mass., January 1998).

74. Quote from Indira Gandhi; ibid., 1.

75. Ibid., 4.

76. This is in contrast to on-patent drug markets, where manufacturing costs are a small component of the price. As one multinational corporation subsidiary executive pointed out, "While the availability of strong intellectual property protection was necessary, other considerations, like tax advantages, were at least as important in choosing a manufacturing location for on-patent drugs." Ibid., 18.

77. Lee Branstetter, Raymond Fisman, and C. Fritz Foley, "Do Stronger Intellectual Property Rights Increase International Technology Transfer? Empirical Evidence from U.S. Firm-Level Data" (working paper, Columbia University, December 2002).

78. Ibid., 31.

79. Ibid., 24.

80. That is, firms with larger patent portfolios saw annual royalty payments increase by around 17 percent more than firms with smaller portfolios. Ibid., 26.

81. Employment increases 9 percent, sales increase 34 percent, costs increase 21 percent, and return on assets increase 2 percentage points post reform. Ibid., 27.

82. Ibid., 29.

83. Ibid., 5.

84. Note that not all Indian research on previously patented drugs is strictly imitative. Adapting these drugs to the varying climates and spotty storage facilities in developing nations is an important part of transferring them from the United States and Europe. Jean Lanjouw, "The Introduction of Pharmaceutical Product Patents in India: Heartless Exploitation of the Poor and Suffering?" 21, note 13. Cited in note 73.

85. Griliches, "Productivity, R & D, and the Data Constraint," 2. Cited in note 1.

86. Ibid., 2.

87. For more on quality-adjusted pricing for computer products, see Ernst R. Berndt and Zvi Griliches, "Price Indexes for Microcomputers: An Exploratory Study," in Price Measurements and Their Uses, ed. M. E. Manser, M. F. Foss, and A. H. Young, NBER Studies in Income and Wealth, vol. 57 (Chicago: University of Chicago Press, 1993), 63–93.

88. For more on pharmaceutical price indices, see Zvi Griliches and Iain A. Cockburn, "Generics and New Goods in Pharmaceutical Price Indexes" (working paper no. 4272, NBER, Cambridge, Mass., 1993).

89. Griliches, "Productivity, R & D, and the Data Constraint," 9.

90. Andrei Shleifer, "The New Comparative Economics," NBER Reporter, Fall 2002, available at http://www.nber.org/reporter/fall02/newEconomics.html.

3

Software Patents: Good News or Bad News?

Stuart J. H. Graham and David C. Mowery

Although measures and definitions of "software patents" vary, virtually all analyses (including data presented in this chapter) agree that patenting in this field has grown since the early 1980s. Controversy over the validity and economic consequences of software patents also has grown during this period. Software patents have been criticized for their poor quality, their chilling effects on innovation, and the reduction in R & D spending in the software industry. In this chapter, we review some of these controversies, emphasizing the paucity of strong evidence to support any of these contentions. Evidence also is lacking, however, in support of the argument that patents are essential to innovation and technological progress in computer software, a technological field in which innovation proceeded apace for at least thirty years before patenting began to grow rapidly. Indeed, it is difficult to understand the causes of recent growth in software patenting without a brief historical review of the development of the U.S. software industry and (of no less importance) the development of judicial decisions on the validity and coverage of patents and other legal devices for protecting software-related intellectual property. Nevertheless, the growth of software patenting highlights the difficulties faced by the U.S. patent system in dealing with new areas of patenting, especially when increased patenting flows as much from change in the legal strength of patents or industry structure as from the development of a new field of technology.

We begin by discussing the general issues and evidence (or lack thereof) concerning the role of patents in technological innovation. This section is followed by a brief survey of the development of the U.S. computer software industry, as well as a discussion of the complex evolution of judicial decisions on the validity of patents and other legal forms of intellectual property protection for software during the 1980s and 1990s. We then discuss our data on trends in patenting, focusing in particular on packaged software. A discussion of the complex issues of patent "quality" is followed by a conclusion and consideration of policy implications.

Our basic conclusions can be summarized as follows: Although patents and other forms of legal protection for intellectual property have assumed greater importance in the software industry since the early 1980s, the long history of innovation in the sector makes it difficult to argue that strong patent protection is indispensable for software innovation. And it is possible that various forms of "strategic patenting" could impede innovation in this technology. Nevertheless, strong evidence of such impediments is lacking. Moreover, the appropriate policy response to a software patenting "problem" is not obvious—*sui generis* protection may create as many problems as it resolves. The growth of software patenting and software patenting controversies, however, raise broader issues concerning the weaknesses of the "quality control" procedures within the U.S. Patent and Trademark Office's administrative reviews of patent applications. These procedural weaknesses affect patenting across the board, although their effects are likely to be most significant in new technological fields for which patent-based prior art is relatively scarce.

Patents and Innovation

To highlight some of the key policy issues in any discussion of patenting in software, we begin with a short review of recent work on the links between patents and innovation. Despite the recent upsurge in research on the economics of innovation and intellectual property, surprisingly little new empirical research provides answers to such critical issues as the importance of patents for innovation. Instead, the evidence is mixed and ambiguous at best.

Mazzoleni and Nelson[1] provide an excellent overview of the economic evidence concerning the roles of patents in innovation and argue that economists have highlighted four key functions of the patent system in the innovation process:

1. Providing incentives for inventive activity, by enabling inventors to capture the returns to their investments of funds and time in inventive activity.

2. Providing incentives for the commercial development of inventions, by enabling investors in commercialization to capture the returns to their investments in technology development and supporting markets for well-defined pieces of intellectual property.

3. Providing incentives for inventors to disclose technical details of their inventions through publication of patents.

4. Enabling the orderly development of "follow-on" inventions.

The authors note that these arguments have figured prominently in the series of U.S. policy initiatives dating back to the 1980s that have strengthened patent-holder rights in domestic and international markets.

But Mazzoleni and Nelson also emphasize the weak evidentiary basis for strong claims about the contributions of patents to invention and innovation. Surveys and other empirical work,[2] for example, suggest that the "invention incentive" effect of patents is limited in most industries other than pharmaceuticals and scientific instruments; typically other mechanisms or strategies are rated more highly by R & D managers as means to capture the returns to invention. The "development incentives" created by patents also are not well founded on solid evidence, although arguments concerning the benefits of markets for intellectual property and licensing influenced the passage of important pieces of legislation such as the Bayh-Dole Act of 1980.[3] Clearly, in some industries (e.g., biotechnology), stronger patents have supported the growth of markets for intellectual property that in turn created a vertically specialized industry structure. But these examples are most abundant in the biomedical field, and there is not much evidence that the vertically specialized industry structure now characteristic of computer hardware and software owes much to the development of strong intellectual property rights. The "disclosure effects" of patent publication have been less closely examined, as have those of the broad patents deemed most helpful to the commercial exploitation of "prospects" for the creation of a series of inventions. Merges and Nelson, however, argue that broad patents may have a chilling effect on the entry by other inventors into the exploitation of broad technological opportunities.[4] And Scotchmer and Green suggest that difficulties in developing efficient licensing arrangements for such broad patents may impede follow-on inventive activity by parties other than the original inventor.[5] Overall, however, the evidence here too is ambiguous.

Another issue that figures prominently in any discussion of software patents is patent "quality"; that is, are patents being issued for inventions that genuinely meet the criteria of nonobviousness and utility, or do weak procedures for review of patent applications result in the issue of patents whose quality is dubious or uncertain, pending a court challenge? As we note in this chapter, the processes through which patent applications are reviewed necessarily are backward looking, since they focus on prior art, much of which is embodied in previously issued patents. New fields of inventive activity, therefore, pose significant challenges to patent review procedures. Some of these problems can be overcome through procedures that enable "interested parties" to challenge patents immediately after issue through administrative procedures, such as the "opposition proceedings" of the European Patent Office and numerous European nations. But, in the absence of well-developed administrative procedures for challenges to patent validity, litigation provides a costly and time-consuming alternative that may prolong uncertainty over patent validity and have a chilling effect on incentives to invent, markets for intellectual property, and investment in "follow-on" inventions.

The links between patenting and innovation thus remain hazy in fields of technology other than the biomedical sector, although little if any of this research has included software within the sample of industries or technologies examined. Our discussion of trends in software patenting and innovative activity during the 1978–2003 period provides little evidence that increased software patenting reflects much more than the response of managers to the greater ease in obtaining software patents. Moreover, as we pointed out earlier, vertical specialization in this industry predates the era of stronger patent protection. At the same time, there is little evidence that stronger patents have had a chilling effect on innovation in this field, nor do we find strong evidence that "follow-on" invention is being impeded by increased fragmentation or complexity in the intellectual property rights environment. Nor do we find that the "quality" of software patents has declined precipitously during this period, although the relatively weak procedures within the U.S. patent system for administrative challenges to patent validity mean that the problem of "junk patents" should not be minimized.

The Historical Development of the Computer Software Industry

The growth of the global computer software industry has been marked by at least four distinct eras spanning the 1945–present period. The first era (1945–65) covers the development and commercialization of the computer. The gradual adoption of "standard" computer architectures in the 1950s supported the emergence of software that could operate on more than one type of computer or in more than one computer installation. In the United States, the introduction of the IBM 650 in the 1950s, followed by the even more dominant IBM 360 in the 1960s, provided a large market for standard operating systems and application programs. The emergence of a large installed base of a single mainframe architecture occurred first and to the greatest extent in the United States. Nonetheless, most of the software for mainframe computers during this period was produced by their manufacturers and users.

During the second era (1965–78), independent software vendors (ISVs) began to appear. During the late 1960s, producers of mainframe computers "unbundled" their software product offerings from their hardware products, separating the pricing and distribution of hardware and software. This development provided opportunities for entry by independent producers of standard and custom operating systems, as well as independent suppliers of applications software for mainframes. Unbundling occurred in the United States first and progressed further in the United States and Western Europe than in the Japanese software industry.

Although independent suppliers of software began to enter the market in significant numbers in the early 1970s, computer manufacturers and users remained important sources of both custom and standard software in Japan, Western Europe, and the United States during this period. Some computer "service bureaus" that had provided users with operating services and programming solutions began to unbundle their services from their software, providing yet another cohort of entrants into the independent development and sale of traded software. Sophisticated users of computer systems, especially users of mainframe computers, also created solutions for their applications and operating system needs. A number of leading suppliers of traded software in Japan, Western Europe, and the United States were founded by computer specialists formerly employed by major mainframe users.

During the third era (1978–93), the development and diffusion of the desktop computer produced explosive growth in the traded software industry. Once again, the United States was the "first mover" in this transformation, and the U.S. domestic market became the largest single market for packaged software. Rapid adoption of the desktop computer in the United States supported the early emergence of a few "dominant designs" in desktop computer architecture, creating the first mass market for packaged software. The independent vendors that entered the desktop software industry in the United States were largely new to the industry. Few of the major suppliers of desktop software came from the ranks of the leading independent producers of mainframe and minicomputer software, and mainframe and minicomputer ISVs are still minor factors in desktop software.

Rapid diffusion of low-cost desktop computer hardware, combined with the emergence of a few "dominant designs" for this architecture, eroded vertical integration between hardware and software producers and opened up opportunities for ISVs. Interestingly, however, this trend of increasingly vertical specialization was established during a period of relatively weak formal protection for software-related intellectual property. Declines in the costs of computing technology continually expanded the array of potential applications for computers; many of these applications rely on software solutions for their realization. A growing installed base of ever-cheaper computers has been an important source of dynamism and entry into the traded software industry, because the expansion of market niches in applications has outrun the ability of established computer manufacturers and major producers of packaged software to supply them.[6]

The packaged computer software industry now has a cost structure that resembles that of the publishing and entertainment industries much more than that of custom software—the returns to a "hit" product are enormous and production costs are low. And, like these other industries, the growth of a mass market for software has elevated the importance of formal intellectual property rights.

The fourth era in the development of the software industry (1994–present) has been dominated by the growth of networking among desktop computers within enterprises through local area networks linked to a server or the Internet, which links millions of users. Networking has opened opportunities for the emergence of new software market segments (for example, the operating system software that is currently installed in desktop computers may reside on the network or the server), the emergence of new "dominant designs," and potentially, the erosion of currently dominant software firms' positions. Like previous eras in the industry's development, the growth of network users and applications has been more rapid in the United States than in other industrial economies, and U.S. firms have maintained dominant positions in these markets.[7]

How has the growth of the Internet changed the economics of intellectual property protection in the software industry? At least three different effects are apparent thus far in the Internet's development. First, the widespread diffusion of the Internet has created new channels for low-cost distribution and marketing of packaged software, reducing the barriers to entry into the packaged software industry based on the dominance of established distribution channels by large packaged software firms. In this respect, the Internet expands the possibilities for rapid penetration of markets by a "hit" packaged software product (in the jargon of the software industry, a "killer app"), which enhances the economic importance of protection for these types of intellectual property. The Internet also is an important factor in the growth of patents on software-embodied "business methods," many of which concern tools or routines employed by on-line marketers of goods and services.

But the Internet also has provided new impetus to the diffusion and rapid growth of a very different type of software, "open source" software. Although so-called shareware has been important throughout the development of the software industry, the Internet's ability to support rapid, low-cost distribution of new software and (crucially) the centralized collection and incorporation into that software of improvements from users has made possible such widely used operating systems as Linux and Apache.[8] The Internet thus increased the importance of formal protection of some types of software-related intellectual property, while simultaneously supporting the growth of open source software, which does not rely on such formal instruments of IP protection.

The Evolution of Intellectual Property Rights Policy and Practice in the U.S. Software Industry

This study is concerned primarily with intellectual property rights in software that combine some grant of limited monopoly in exchange for an element of disclosure or public use. As such, it is appropriate to examine copyright and patent protection, since software has been brought underneath the umbrella of each of these regimes during the last several decades. But software innovators also have obtained legal protections for intellectual property by using trade secrets,[9] legal assertions of misappropriation,[10] trademark,[11] and even the Semiconductor Chip Protection Act.[12]

Copyright. Copyright protection for software innovation was singled out by policymakers during the 1970s as the preferred means for protecting software-related intellectual property.[13] In its 1979 report, the National Commission on New Technological Uses of Copyrighted Works (CONTU), charged with making recommendations to Congress regarding software protection, chose copyright as the most appropriate form of protection for computer software.[14] Congress adopted the commission's position when it wrote "computer program" into the Copyright Act in 1980.[15]

The federal judiciary's application of copyright to software in the aftermath of the CONTU initially promised strong protection for inventors. *Apple Computer, Inc. v. Franklin Computer Corp.*[16] is an early, important case of copyright litigation in packaged software. Although the federal judiciary had long held that copyright protected only "expression" in works,[17] the Court in *Apple Computer* held that Apple's precise code was protected by its copyright. This decision strengthened copyright protection considerably, making it possible for one firm's copyrighted software to block the innovative efforts of others. Subsequent decisions—the so-called look-and-feel cases—extended traditional copyright protection of "expression" to such "nonliteral" elements of software as structure, sequence, and organization.[18]

Subsequent court decisions, however, narrowed the protection provided by copyright for software-related intellectual property. The sweeping interpretation of copyright protection in the *Apple Computer* case was narrowed and weakened in a series of copyright infringement cases brought by Lotus Development. The *Borland* decision weakened the strong protection for software inventions provided by *Apple Computer v. Franklin Computer*, and, along with other decisions affirming the strength of software patents, may have contributed to increased reliance by some U.S. software firms on patents in the 1990s.

Patent. In contrast to copyright, federal court decisions since 1980 have broadened and strengthened the economic value of software patents. In the cases of *Diamond v. Diehr*[19] and *Diamond v. Bradley*,[20] both decided in 1981, the Supreme Court announced a more liberal rule that permitted the patenting of software algorithms, strengthening patent protection for software.[21] The economic value of these patents was highlighted in several high-profile cases during the 1990s. For example, a 1994 court decision found Microsoft liable for patent infringement and awarded $120 million in damages to Stac Electronics. The damages award was hardly a crippling blow to Microsoft, but the firm's infringing product had to be withdrawn from the market temporarily, compounding the financial and commercial consequences of the decision.[22]

As the USPTO adopted a more favorable posture toward applications for software patents, the quality of issued patents in an area of technology in which patents historically had not been used to cover major innovations was called into question. The celebrated "multimedia" patent issued by the USPTO to Compton Encyclopedias in 1993 is one example of these difficulties. On November 15, 1993, Compton's Newmedia announced that it had won a "fundamental" patent for its multimedia software that rapidly fetched images and sound.[23] The patent was quite broad, covering "a database search system that retrieves multimedia information in a flexible, user-friendly system. The search system uses a multimedia database consisting of text, picture, audio and animated data. That database is searched through multiple graphical and textual entry paths."[24]

Compton's president, Stanley Frank, suggested that the firm did not want to slow growth in the multimedia industry, but he did "want the public to recognize Compton's Newmedia as the pioneer in this industry, promote a standard that can be used by every developer, and be compensated for the investments we have made." Armed with this patent, Compton's traveled to Comdex, the computer industry trade show, to detail its licensing terms to competitors, which involved payment of a 1 percent royalty for a nonexclusive license.[25]

Compton's appearance at Comdex launched a political controversy that culminated in an unusual event—the U.S. Patent and Trademark Office reconsidered and invalidated the Compton's patent. On December 17, 1993, the USPTO ordered an internal reexamination of Compton's patent because, in the words of Commissioner Lehman, "this patent caused a great deal of angst in the industry."[26] On March 28, 1994, the USPTO released a preliminary statement declaring that "[a]ll claims in Compton's multimedia patent issued in August 1993 have been rejected on the grounds that they lack 'novelty' or are obvious in view of prior art."[27] This declaration was confirmed by the USPTO in November of 1994.[28]

Similar concerns over the validity or quality of software-related patents appeared in the field of "business methods" patents, a field of patenting that grew rapidly in the wake of the 1998 decision of the Court of Appeals for the Federal Circuit (CAFC) affirming the validity of a "business methods" software patent in *State Street Bank v. Signature Financial Group*.[29] USPTO Commissioner Dickinson noted, in March 2000, that the number of applications for such patents had expanded from 1,275 in fiscal 1998 to 2,600 in fiscal 1999, resulting in the issue of 600 business methods patents in 1999. As in the case of the Compton's patent, concerns over the quality of Internet-based "business methods" patents reflect the lack of patent-based prior art available for review by USPTO examiners.[30]

Political reactions to the surge in business methods patents and the controversy surrounding their validity were swift and involved both Congress and the USPTO. In late 1999, Congress passed the American Inventor Protection Act (AIPA). The AIPA was originally drafted to revise the U.S. patent system to be consistent with the WTO agreements that concluded the Uruguay Round of trade negotiations, but additional provisions were added specifically to address the business methods patent controversy. The act includes a "first-to-invent" defense against infringement claims, protecting defendants who can show that they were practicing the relevant method or art one year or more prior to the filing of the patent application against infringement suits.

Administrative responses to the business methods controversy included the USPTO's Business Methods Patent Initiative, unveiled in the spring of 2000. The initiative included several provisions:

1. Hiring more than 500 new patent examiners specializing in software, computer, and business methods applications.

2. Tripling the number of examiners assigned to examine applications in Class 705, the primary locus of business methods patenting activity.

3. Expanding the number of nonpatent "prior art" databases to which these examiners have access.

4. Requiring that nonpatent and foreign prior art be searched systematically for all applications in Class 705.

5. Requiring examination of all applications in Class 705 by a second examiner in addition to the primary examiner assigned the application.

This administrative initiative raised the level of scrutiny devoted to business methods patent applications and may have reduced the rate of issue of new patents in this class. The USPTO reported in 2001 that the number of examiners assigned to business methods patents increased from 45 at the beginning of fiscal 2000 to 82 by the end of fiscal 2001. The same report predicted that roughly 10,000 applications would be filed in Class 705, which covers most business methods patents, in fiscal 2001, an increase of nearly fourfold since fiscal 1999. But the USPTO issued approximately 433 patents in Class 705 in fiscal 2001, a decrease of more than 25 percent from the number issued in this class in fiscal 1999.[31] The lags involved in review of patent applications (eighteen months to two years) and the rapid growth in applications during fiscal 1999–2001 mean that the number of business methods patents issued by the USPTO almost certainly will increase in the future. Nevertheless, the drop in the number of issued business methods patents during 1998–2001 in the face of swelling applications suggests that the intensified scrutiny of applications in this class may indeed have reduced the rate of issue of business patents somewhat.

The economic significance and validity of U.S. business methods patents ultimately will be determined through litigation.[32] The possibility nonetheless exists that the global nature of the markets in which business methods patents are applied, especially those that rely on the Internet for their operation, may limit the proliferation of "junk patents." Given the footloose nature of the Internet (an Internet enterprise can be established virtually anywhere in the world that has a reasonably well-developed infrastructure), global recognition of Internet-based business methods patents may be necessary to establish their economic value. At present, most European patent systems do not grant validity to business methods patents that do not have a "technical effect."[33] The precise meaning of this distinction is subject to considerable debate and interpretation, suggesting that at least some but by no means all business methods patents issued in the United States will be upheld as valid within Europe. The value of many U.S. business methods patents therefore may be limited, although much uncertainty remains concerning their validity in foreign jurisdictions.

Patenting Trends in the U.S. Software Industry, 1987–2003

This section examines trends in U.S. software patenting during 1987–2003, focusing on the product areas we believe have been most affected by changes in the legal treatment of software patents: packaged software. As our previous paper emphasizes, no widely accepted definition of *software patent* exists, and the problem of identifying software patents is made no easier by USPTO changes in patent classification schemes.[34] Other researchers have chosen to define a *software patent* by reference to certain key words in the patent disclosure,[35] but we rely instead on the classification decisions of USPTO patent examiners. In contrast to our previous paper, which relied exclusively on the International Patent Classifications (IPCs) issued by the World Intellectual Property Organization (WIPO), in this chapter we use both the IPC and the independent U.S. classifications maintained by the USPTO to identify software patents.

One difficulty that arises when using these two patent office classifications is the rapid growth in the number of software-related USPTO patents during the period of this analysis. Because we are interested in analyzing changes over time in the number of software patents, we seek to insulate our sample from any "reclassifications" of patents from "all other" to a "software-related" category. Such an analysis is made more difficult by the USPTO's unannounced reclassifications, although it is aided by the systematic reclassifications announced in the IPC. To eliminate the impact of reclassifications, we use a "snapshot" in time of the U.S. classifications for all U.S.-issued patents, as well as an alternative sampling technique based on IPCs that includes only subclasses that existed throughout 1987–2003.

Using the USPTO's Cassis database, we collected data on all patents issued in the United States in 1987–2003, relying on the USPTO classification scheme as of December 2003, with patents from previous years updated to reflect current USPTO classifications, thus allowing us to compare trends in patenting over time. We concentrated on the following year-end 2003 USPTO classifications:

Class 345: Computer Graphics Processing, Operator Interface Processing, and Selective Visual Display Systems

Class 358: Facsimile and Static Presentation Processing

Class 382: Image Analysis

Class 704: Data Processing: Speech Signal Processing, Linguistics, Language Translation, and Audio Compression/Decompression

Class 707: Data Processing: Database and File Management or Data Structures

Class 709: Electrical Computers and Digital Processing Systems: Multiple Computer or Process

Class 715: Data Processing: Presentation Processing of Document

Class 710: Electrical Computers and Digital Data Processing Systems: Input/Output

Class 711: Electrical Computers and Digital Processing Systems: Memory

Class 713: Electrical Computers and Digital Processing Systems: Support

Class 714: Error Detection/Correction and Fault Detection/ Recovery

Class 717: Data Processing: Software Development, Installation, and Management

These classifications were identified by examining U.S. patenting in the years 1987–2003 by the six largest U.S. producers of personal computer software, based on their calendar 2000 revenues.[36] These patent classes account for 65.7 percent of the more than 3,800 patents assigned to the one hundred largest packaged-software firms identified by *Softletter*, a trade newsletter, in its 2001 tabulation.[37] These twelve classes account for 67.9 percent of the patenting of the "top 6" firms, while these firms account for 88.4 percent of the patenting of the *Softletter* "top 100." Table 3-1 contains data on the distribution of the patents in this sample among the twelve USPTO classes just listed.

Employing the same sample of patents from the "top 6" personal computer software firms, we generated an alternative definition of a "software" patent for comparison purposes, based on the International Patent Classification. We focused on the following classes:

G06F Electric Digital Data Processing

3/ Input arrangements for transferring data to be processed into a form capable of being handled by the computer . . .

9/ Arrangements for programme control . . .

11/ Error detection; Error correction; Monitoring . . .

12/ Accessing, addressing, or allocating within memory systems or architectures . . .

TABLE 3-1

PATENTING BY THE *SOFTLETTER 100*, BY USPTO PATENT CLASS, 1987–2003

(total patents = 3,891)

U.S. Patent Class	Patent Count	Share of All Firm Patents (%)	Cumulative Total (%)
345	730	18.8	18.8
707	624	16.0	34.8
709	363	9.3	44.1
382	157	4.0	48.2
713	141	3.6	51.8
704	125	3.2	55.0
717	118	3.0	58.0
714	85	2.2	60.2
711	80	2.1	62.3
710	59	1.5	63.8
358	52	1.3	65.1
715	25	0.6	65.8

SOURCE: Authors' data analysis of *Softletter 100* publications and issued U.S. patents.

13/ Interconnection of, or transfer of information or other signals between, memories, input/output devices, or central processing units

15/ Digital computers in general . . .

17/ Digital computing or data processing equipment or methods, specially adapted for specific functions

G06K Recognition of Data; Presentation of Data; Record Carriers; Handling Record Carriers

9/ Methods or arrangements for reading or recognising printed or written characters or for recognising patterns

G06T Image Data Processing or Generation, in General

11/ Two dimensional (2D) image generation, e.g. from a description to a bit-mapped image

TABLE 3-2

PATENTING BY THE *SOFTLETTER 100*, BY INTERNATIONAL PATENT CLASS, 1995–2003

(total patents = 3,775)

Int'l Patent Class	Patent Count	Share of All Firm Patents (%)	Cumulative Total (%)
G06F 17	796	21.1	21.1
G06F 9	426	11.3	32.4
G06F 15	424	11.2	43.6
G06F 13	259	6.9	50.5
G06F 3	210	5.6	56.0
G09G 5	166	4.4	60.4
G06F 12	145	3.8	64.3
G06K 9	144	3.8	68.1
G06F 11	126	3.3	71.4
G06T 11	86	2.3	73.7

SOURCE: Authors' data analysis of *Softletter 100* publications and issued U.S. patents.

G09G Educating; Cryptography; Display; Advertising; Seals

5/ Control arrangements or circuits for visual indicators common to cathode-ray tube indicators . . .

These patent classes account for 73.6 percent of the more than 3,800 patents assigned during 1995–2003 to the 100 largest packaged-software firms identified by *Softletter*, a trade newsletter, in its 2001 tabulation, and 74 percent of the patenting in these years of the "top 6" firms from which the classification was generated. Table 3-2 provides data on the breakdown of this patent sample among these ten IPC classes.

These patent classes are drawn from classification editions 6 and 7 of the IPC, effective on January 1, 1995, and January 1, 2000, respectively. Since these classes exist throughout the entire 1995–2003 period, they provide us with a useful basis for comparison against our USPTO classification definition, which is based on a "snapshot" of current USPTO activities in December 2003.

Neither of our definitional schemes covers all software patents. They do, however, provide longitudinal coverage of a particularly dynamic and important segment of the overall software industry, inasmuch as the market for packaged software worldwide represents some 50 percent of the total software and software-services industry output.[38] The data in figure 3-1 indicate that the share of all U.S. patents accounted for by patents in both the USPTO classes and the IPC classifications we identified grew sharply through 1999, although growth in patenting in these classes slowed during 2000–2003. USPTO-classification "software" patents grew from 2.1 percent to 7.4 percent of all issued U.S. patents between 1987 and 1998, and the share of patents in these twelve U.S. classes has remained between 6.9 and 7.5 percent of overall patenting during 1999–2003. This pattern is mirrored in IPC-defined "software" patenting, with substantial growth in the share of U.S. patenting (3.9 to 6.7 percent) from 1995 to 1999, but no discernible growth thereafter, with shares fluctuating between 6.3 and 7 percent between 1999 and 2003. This slowdown in the rate of growth in "software" patenting as a share of total U.S. patenting occurs in virtually every class in both the U.S.-class and IPC-classification schemes.[39]

There are several potential explanations for the slowdown in software patent growth, relative to overall U.S. patenting, after 1999. In other work, we noted that 1995 changes in the legal patent term of protection (changing the term of protection from seventeen years from date of application to twenty years from date of issue) created strong incentives for patent applicants to pursue "continuations" in their applications, which (among other advantages) enabled applicants to extend the period of secrecy surrounding their application.[40] Since software-patent applicants made extensive use of continuations, it is possible that a large number of applications were filed immediately prior to the 1995 changes in patent term (whose effects on applicants' incentives to pursue continuations have been intensified by more-recent requirements to publish many patents within eighteen months of application), contributing to a surge in issued patents during 1997–99. It is also possible, however, that the accumulation of experience by USPTO examiners in dealing with software-patent applications, as well as the expanding body of patent-based prior art on which examiners rely in part, led to lower rates of issue for software patent applications filed after 1995. The fluctuations in growth

FIGURE 3-1

SOFTWARE PATENTS' SHARE OF ALL ISSUED U.S. PATENTS, 1987–2003[a]

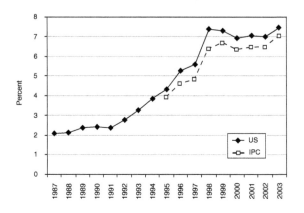

SOURCE: Authors' data analysis of *Softletter 100* publications and issued U.S. patents.
a. Comparing two definitions: U.S. classification and international patent classification.

in software patents do not appear to be associated with fluctuations in the "pendency" of patent applications (the length of time required to review and grant or deny patent applications), since the average pendency of applications for issued software patents, which is greater than the average for all patents, has increased steadily through the 1995–2003 period.[41]

Software-Related Patenting by Packaged Software and Electronic Systems Firms, 1987–2003. In this section, we analyze patenting by U.S. software firms during 1987–2003, focusing on leading U.S. packaged software firms identified by *Softletter* in its 2001 tabulation of the one hundred largest U.S. packaged software firms (based on revenues). We are particularly interested in the behavior of firms' "patent propensity" (patents per R & D dollar) over time, and the R & D spending of these firms is far more likely to be devoted primarily to software development than the software patenting of electronic-systems firms that do not separately report software-related R & D investment. We also focus on these firms because the changes in the legal and policy environment discussed earlier may have had a more substantial effect on these companies.

FIGURE 3-2

LARGE PACKAGED-SOFTWARE FIRMS' PATENTS, AS A SHARE OF ALL
U.S.-ISSUED SOFTWARE PATENTS, 1987–2003[a]

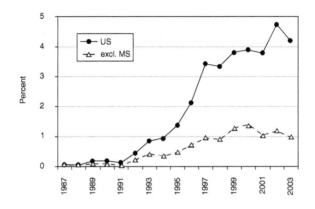

SOURCE: Authors' data analysis of *Softletter 100* publications and issued U.S. patents.
a. Comparison: U.S. software patenting by 100 largest packaged-software firms as share of all software patents issued, including and excluding Microsoft.

Using the USPTO-classification definition of *software*, figure 3-2 displays trends during 1987–2003 in the share of all U.S. software patents held by the 100 largest U.S. packaged software firms, including and excluding the largest player in the industry, Microsoft. Figure 3-2 demonstrates that these firms increased their share of overall software patenting during the 1987–2003 period, from less than 0.06 percent in of all software patents in 1988 to nearly 4.75 percent in 2002, declining to 4.13 percent of software patents in 2003. Eliminating Microsoft from the figure reveals more modest growth, with the share growing from less than 0.06 percent in 1987 to 1.35 percent in 2000 and declining to 1 percent in 2003. Similar to figure 3-1, the data in figure 3-2 suggest rapid growth in software patenting through the late 1990s, followed by no growth or declines after 2000.

Although patenting by large packaged-software firms has grown since the late 1980s, it is interesting to note that electronic systems firms account for a much larger share of software patenting as we define it (a definition that weights packaged-software patents more heavily than the schema developed

FIGURE 3-3

LARGE SYSTEMS FIRMS' SOFTWARE PATENTS, AS A SHARE OF
ALL SOFTWARE PATENTS, 1987–2003[a]

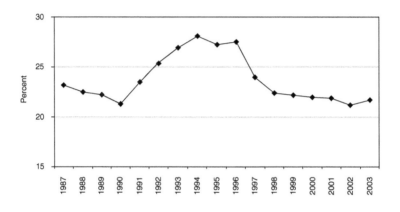

SOURCE: Authors' data analysis of *Softletter 100* publications and issued U.S. patents.
a. Weighted average, U.S. software patenting by IBM, Intel, Hewlett-Packard, Motorola, National Semiconductor, NEC, Digital Equipment, Compaq Computer, Hitachi, Fujitsu, Texas Instruments, and Toshiba).

by Bessen and Hunt[42]). Both our USPTO and IPC classification schemes show that the share of overall "software" patents accounted for by large electronic systems firms (IBM, Intel, Hewlett-Packard, Motorola, National Semiconductor, NEC, Digital Equipment Corporation, Compaq, Hitachi, Fujitsu, Texas Instruments, and Toshiba) considerably exceeds the share of these patents assigned to specialist packaged-software firms. Figure 3-3 depicts the share of software patents assigned to our sample of twelve electronics systems firms, which fluctuates between a low of 21 percent in 1990 and a high of 28 percent in 1994, before falling to 21–23 percent of all software patenting for 1998–2003.[43]

We also calculated the share of all patents issued to these firms classified by the USPTO examiners into our defined U.S. software patent classes during 1987–2003. Figure 3-4 displays the time trend for the software patent share within these twelve firms' patent portfolios during 1987–2003. Software patents' share of overall firm patents increased during the 1987–2003 period for all these firms from roughly 14 percent in 1987 to

FIGURE 3-4

LARGE SYSTEMS FIRMS' SOFTWARE PATENTS,
AS A SHARE OF FIRM PATENTS, 1987–2003[a]

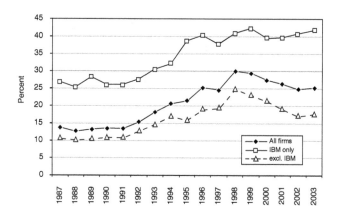

SOURCE: Authors' data analysis of *Softletter 100* publications and issued U.S. patents.
a. Weighted average, U.S. software patenting by IBM, Intel, Hewlett-Packard, Motorola, National Semiconductor, NEC, Digital Equipment, Compaq Computer, Hitachi, Fujitsu, Texas Instruments, and Toshiba.

25 percent of their overall patent portfolios by 2003. Even more striking, however, is the level and growth of software patenting by IBM, which increases its software patenting from 27 percent of its overall patenting in 1987 to 42 percent in 2003. In contrast to the software patenting of the other eleven systems firms, IBM's share of software patents in its annual patenting increased through 2003.

Changes in the "Patent Propensity" of Packaged-Software Firms, 1987–2003. The data presented thus far suggest that software patenting has grown during at least the first part of the 1987–2003 period but provide no information on the "intensity" of patenting effort by the firms obtaining software patents. Obviously, the interpretation of an increase in software patenting proportionate to growth in software-related R & D investment differs from a finding that patenting is growing more rapidly than R & D investment. The first case may constitute evidence of intensified innovative effort in software in response to stronger patents. The second case suggests that

FIGURE 3-5

TOP FIFTEEN PACKAGED-SOFTWARE FIRMS' SOFTWARE PATENT PROPENSITY,
FIRMS' PATENTS PER R & D EXPENDITURE, 1987–2002[a]

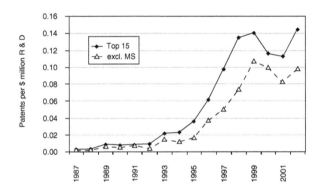

SOURCE: Authors' data analysis of *Softletter 100* publications and issued U.S. patents.
a. Comparing Microsoft, Adobe Systems, Novell, Intuit, Autodesk, Symantec, Network Associates,
Citrix, Macromedia, Great Plains, RealNetworks, Borland (Inprise), SPSS, Phoenix Technologies, and
Santa Cruz Operation with top fourteen firms, same excluding Microsoft.

stronger patents lead to more patenting relative to software-specific R & D
investment. A third possibility, which cannot be ruled out, is that there is little if any relationship among software-related R & D investment, software-
related innovation, and software patenting. We examine the relationship
between patenting and software-related R & D investment for the firms for
which the latter data are available (unfortunately, we lack these data for most
of our electronic systems firms) during 1987–2002.

The list of packaged-software firms provided by *Softletter* allows us to analyze the large packaged-software firms' "propensity to patent," measured as
the ratio of patents to constant-dollar R & D spending, during the
1987–2002 period (figures 3-5 and 3-6).[44] Figure 3-5 displays data on trends
in the weighted-average patent propensity for the fifteen largest U.S.-based
packaged-software firms.[45] These firms include the largest fifteen publicly
traded firms by year 2000 revenue, as follows: Microsoft, Adobe Systems,
Novell, Intuit, Autodesk, Symantec, Network Associates, Citrix Systems,
Macromedia, Great Plains Software, RealNetworks, Borland (Inprise), SPSS,

FIGURE 3-6

**LARGEST PACKAGED-SOFTWARE FIRMS' SOFTWARE PATENT PROPENSITY,
FIRMS' PATENTS PER R & D EXPENDITURE, 1987–2002[a]**

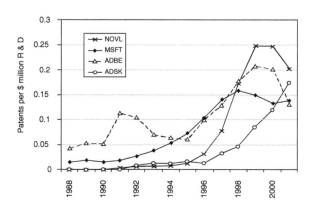

SOURCE: Authors' data analysis of *Softletter 100* publications and issued U.S. patents.
a. Three-year moving averages, comparing Novell, Microsoft, Adobe Systems, and Autodesk.

Phoenix Technologies, and SCO (Santa Cruz Operation). Figure 3-5 also compares the patent propensity of Microsoft with the aggregate propensity of the other fourteen largest software firms (Microsoft accounted for more than 75 percent of these firms' U.S. patents issued during 2000–03).

Figure 3-5 demonstrates that patenting per R & D dollar grew during the 1987–2002 period, in spite of a downturn during 2000–2001. This pattern is apparent both in the patent propensity of all fifteen firms and in the sample of firms that excludes Microsoft. The figure suggests that the "propensity to patent" of these firms grew especially rapidly during 1994–2000, a development that may reflect the policy changes (discussed previously) affecting the patent term that came into effect in the United States in 1995. Interestingly, the decline in R & D investment reported by many large packaged-software firms after 2000[46] did not cause further increases in the patent propensity trends depicted in figure 3-5, suggesting a particularly significant drop in the number of patents issued to these firms after 2000. These data for the largest packaged-software firms thus reinforce the descriptive findings of figure 3-2 suggesting that the post-2000 period is one in which patenting of

FIGURE 3-7

COMPARISON OF IBM AND MICROSOFT'S SOFTWARE PATENT PROPENSITY, FIRMS'
SOFTWARE PATENTS PER SOFTWARE R & D EXPENDITURES, 1992–2003a

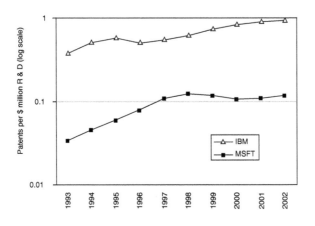

SOURCE: Authors' data analysis of *Softletter 100* publications and issued U.S. patents.
a. Three-year moving averages, patenting limited to each firm's defined software patents.

software declined. Figure 3-6 displays trends in firm-specific patenting
propensities (as three-year moving averages) during 1987–2003 for four of
the largest U.S. personal computer software firms (as identified in the 2001
Softletter rankings of the top one hundred packaged-software firms) with significant patenting activity in 2000.[47] Although the pattern for Microsoft is
noteworthy, given that firm's prominent position in the industry, all three of
the largest packaged-software firms (Microsoft, Novell, and Adobe Systems),
display the same general pattern: growth in patents per R & D dollar during
the years 1987–99 that tapers off after 2000, a period of declining R & D bud-
gets in all but Microsoft. Only Autodesk shows a steady growth in measured
patent propensity throughout the entire 1987–2002 period.

Inasmuch as electronic systems firms appear to account for a larger share
of patenting during the 1987–2003 period than packaged-software specialists, a comparison of patenting propensities between systems and software-
specialist firms would be illuminating. Unfortunately, as we noted earlier, the
absence of detailed line of business reporting of their R & D investments
means that we have data on software-related R & D spending for only one

of the twelve systems firms included in figure 3-3, IBM. Figure 3-7 compares the patent propensities of IBM and Microsoft for the 1992–2003 period. The data in the figure are presented on a log scale and show that IBM's software patenting per software R & D dollar spent is substantially greater than Microsoft's, dominating the packaged-software firm's propensity by a factor approaching or exceeding an order of magnitude (a factor of ten) in every three-year interval. Furthermore, Microsoft's patent propensity "plateaued" at between 0.10 and 0.12 patents per $100 million during the 1996–2003 period, but IBM's continued to grow, climbing from 0.7 patents per $100 million R & D during 1997–1999 to nearly 1 patent per $100 million R & D during 2001–2003.[48] Some of the reported growth in IBM's patent/R & D ratio reflects shrinkage in the firm's reported software R & D budget during 1997–2002, a period of growth for Microsoft R & D investments. Nevertheless, the figure suggests a considerable contrast in the patenting behavior of the largest packaged-software specialist and the largest software producer among U.S. electronic systems firms.

Patent Quality Issues

Despite considerable debate over the issue, there is little compelling evidence of sharp changes in the "quality" of the software patents that have grown considerably in number since 1987. Using data on patent citations, Graham and Mowery found little evidence that the average post-issue citations received by patents issuing to packaged-software or electronics system firms had declined significantly relative to software patents overall.[49] Relying on different evidence, Hunter argues that recent patents in business methods (many of which are embodied in software) were not significantly inferior to other data-processing patents.[50] This evidence is preliminary, and additional research on this issue is needed. It is worth noting, however, that during the 1980s, some leading scholars argued that patents were preferable to copyright as a means of protecting software-related intellectual property, because of the higher "quality threshold" imposed by USPTO for the issue of patents, as well as the limited term of protection provided by patents. Menell's influential 1989 analysis of intellectual property protection of software, written in the wake of the strong judicial interpretation of copyright embodied in *Apple v. Franklin*

Computer Corp., argues that patents had significant advantages over copy-right as a means for protecting computer applications software: "The patent system's threshold requirements for protection—novelty, utility, and nonobviousness—are better tailored than the copyright standard to reward-ing only those innovations that would not be forthcoming without protec-tion."[51] The debate over the quality of software patents[52] centers on precisely these issues: Is the U.S. Patent and Trademark Office able to apply these requirements with sufficient rigor to prevent the issue of low-quality patents?

Here, as elsewhere, however, it is important to avoid confusing forest and trees. New fields of inventive activity almost always pose significant chal-lenges to the USPTO examination system, simply because examiners rely heavily on patent-based prior art. This problem is by no means limited to software, although this field may present some novel twists, because the "patentability" of this particular artifact was endorsed by the U.S. judiciary well after the emergence of a substantial industry populated by inventive firms. The emergence of software patents thus occurred against a backdrop of substantial "prior art," much of which had not been patented.

A lack of efficient, reliable processes for resolving patent validity and ensuring higher patent quality also may slow the pace of invention in fields characterized by "cumulative invention," that is, those in which one inventor's efforts rely on previous technical advances or advances in complementary technologies. But if these previous technical advances are covered by patents of dubious validity or excessive breadth, the costs to inventors of pursuing the inventions that rely on them may be so high as to discourage such "cumula-tive" invention. Alternatively, large numbers of low-quality patents may increase "fragmentation" of property rights covering prior generation or com-plementary technologies, raising the transaction costs for inventors of obtain-ing access (e.g., through licenses) to these technologies. Finally, the issue of a large number of low-quality patents will increase uncertainty among inven-tors concerning the level of protection enjoyed by these related inventions, which in turn will make it more costly and difficult for inventors to build on these related inventions in their own technical advances.

The issuance of low-quality patents also is likely to spur significant increases in patent applications, further straining the already overburdened examination processes of the USPTO. A kind of vicious circle may result, in which cursory examinations of patent applications result in the issue of low-quality patents, which triggers rapid growth in applications, further taxing the limited resources of the USPTO, further limiting the examination of individual applications, and further degrading the quality of patents.

It is important to recognize, therefore, that the "quality issues" raised by software patenting may be unusual but are by no means unique to software. In fact, the U.S. patent system lacks strong administrative procedures for third-party challenges to patents before or immediately after their issue. The primary "quality control" mechanism for patent validity in the U.S. system, of course, is litigation, which is costly and time-consuming, requiring years to resolve the validity of especially contentious (and therefore valuable) patents.

Reexamination, originally envisioned as an alternative to expensive and time-consuming litigation, was created in 1980 as an administrative mechanism for administrative reviews of patent validity that would be less expensive and less time-consuming than litigation. A reexamination permits the patent owner or any other party to request that the USPTO reconsider the issue of a patent, typically based on the disclosure to the Patent Office of some previously undisclosed "new" and relevant piece of prior art. Under the statute, a relevant disclosure must be printed in either a prior patent or prior publication; no other source can serve as grounds for the reexamination.

After being initiated by notification and the payment of a fee to the USPTO, the reexamination goes forward only if the USPTO finds a "substantial new question of patentability" within three months of the request and, having made the determination, notifies the patent owner. The reexamination is an ex parte proceeding between the patent owner and the USPTO that provides limited opportunities for third-party involvement. The examiner remains the final arbiter of the process, and it is not uncommon for the original examiner to be assigned the follow-up reexamination, thus putting the question of whether prior art was overlooked in the hands of the same government official who was responsible for ensuring that no prior art was overlooked in the previous search. A reexamination may result in the cancellation of all or some of the claims in a patent or the confirmation of all or some of the claims. Nothing in the reexamination procedure can expand the scope of the original patent's claims, but claims may be amended or new claims added during the renegotiation between the patent owner and the examiner.

In summary, for parties seeking to invalidate an issued patent, the reexamination procedure involves considerable costs and risks. The filing fee for the reexamination is substantial, and practitioners estimate the average costs of a reexamination at \$10,000–\$100,000, depending on the complexity of the matter. Although the costs of a reexamination are lower than those of litigation (\$1–3 million), the third-party challenger in reexamination is denied a meaningful role in the process, and the patent holder maintains communication with the examining officer, offering amendments or adding new claims during the reexamination. Reexamination may make it more difficult for challengers to prevail in patent-validity litigation, because juries tend to give added weight to reexamined patents. Moreover, the Court of Appeals for the Federal Circuit has indicated that claims confirmed by the reexamining officer present added barriers to a successful contest. As a result, challengers face powerful incentives to forgo reexamination in favor of litigation, a process that may well be more expensive, more time-consuming, and less expert in testing post-issue validity.

Hall et al. compared the operation of the post-issue reexamination and opposition systems for challenging patent validity in the United States and drew some conclusions about the differences between an ex parte system such as is currently found in the United States and an inter partes system used in Europe.[53] First, the U.S. reexamination procedure differs from the European Patent Office (EPO) opposition procedure in virtually all its features. Reexaminations are much less common, with an overall average rate of 0.2 percent, in contrast to the European opposition rate of about 8 percent, and the identity of the party requesting a reexamination is the patent owner in at least 44 percent of the cases, lowering the effective rate even more. This characteristic of reexamination hardly qualifies it as the sort of adversarial procedure that EPO oppositions represent. But EPO oppositions resolve validity challenges more slowly than USPTO reexamination proceedings. Indeed, opposition proceedings in some cases (and almost certainly in important, complex cases with numerous opponents, appeals, etc.) may well take as much time to be resolved as litigation in the U.S. system. Nonetheless, the higher frequency of EPO opposition than U.S. reexamination or litigation is at least consistent with the hypothesis that the opposition process handles many more legal disputes over patent validity than are addressed by the U.S. reexamination process and at a lower cost than the U.S. litigation process.

EPO patent opposition proceedings are more likely to lead to outcomes unfavorable to the patent holder. Patent revocation is much more likely when a patent is opposed in Europe (one in three is revoked) than when a patent is reexamined in the United States (only one in ten is revoked). Combined with the lower probability of reexamination, the overall probability that a patent is revoked via a postgrant administrative challenge is 3 percent in Europe and essentially zero (0.02 percent) in the United States. Conversely, reexamination is more likely than opposition to lead to amendment of the patent, whether or not the patent owner initiated the process. Patent amendment, rather than revocation, is more likely for oppositions in relatively new fields of inventive activity, for more "complex" patents, or for oppositions in which numerous opponents participate.

Conclusion

Spurred by favorable judicial decisions and change in industry structure, software patenting has grown significantly in the United States since the 1980s, although the available data suggest that growth in software patenting may have slowed since approximately 2000. Little evidence suggests that increased patenting has been associated with higher levels of innovation in the U.S. software industry, although little evidence suggests that increased patenting has proven harmful to innovation in this important sector of the "postindustrial" economy. The vertically specialized structure of the U.S. software industry, populated by firms specializing in software only, is a dramatic shift from the vertically integrated structure that characterized the U.S. and global computer industries in the 1960s. But stronger patent protection for software emerged in the 1980s, well after the transformation of this industry structure that began in the late 1960s. The links between stronger formal protection for intellectual property in this industry and the development of its vertically specialized structure thus are weak.

Patenting appears to have grown more rapidly than R & D spending during 1987–99 in those firms for which both software patent data and software-specific R & D investment are available, although here, too, growth has slowed since roughly 2000. But, since the causal links among software-specific R & D investment, software innovation, and software patenting are murky or ambiguous at best, contentions that increased software patenting somehow "causes" declines in R & D investment[54] remain unproven.

Indeed, the most robust conclusion seems to be that of Hall: "[I]ntroducing or strengthening a patent system (lengthening the patent term, broadening subject matter coverage, etc.) unambiguously results in an increase in patenting and in the strategic use of patents. It is much less clear that these changes result in an increase in innovative activity, although they may redirect such activity toward things that are patentable and/or are not subject to being kept secret within the firm."[55]

Electronic systems firms accounted for a larger share of overall software patenting, in our definition, than packaged-software specialist firms during the 1987–2003 period. Moreover, the ratio of patents to software-specific R & D investment for the one large systems firm for which we have reliable data (IBM) suggests a significantly higher "patent propensity" than we observe for the largest packaged-software specialist firm, Microsoft. It is possible, although we have no direct evidence to support this argument, that systems firms are patenting their software-related intellectual property for strategic reasons, such as to support complex cross-licensing agreements similar to those in the semiconductor industry discussed in Hall and Ziedonis.[56] There is less evidence of such cross-licensing agreements among software specialists, although the recent agreement between Microsoft and Sun Microsystems provides one such example.[57] As Hall and Ziedonis note, much of the cross-licensing that provides incentives for extensive patenting by firms is motivated by the prospect or the reality of litigation. Evidence from software patent litigation cited in Graham indicates that packaged-software specialist firms account for a smaller fraction of software patent litigation, by comparison with computer hardware firms and firms from a diverse array of other industries.[58]

One of the thorniest problems in analyzing software patenting, of course, is defining and measuring software patents. The empirical definition employed in this chapter tends to weight packaged-software patents more heavily than definitions employed elsewhere.[59] We used this definition to track trends in patenting by software-specialist firms for which R & D data were available, and it seems likely that the more-expansive definition of *software patents* employed in Bessen and Hunt may categorize as software patents a number of patents in the fields of electronic controls that use "embedded" software in complex hardware systems.[60] But the difficulties of defining and categorizing *software patents* point to a larger challenge to those who advocate prohibitions on software patents or some form of *sui generis* protection: If the definition of a software patent is open to debate and interpretation, how can rules (prohibitions or *sui generis* protection) specific to software inventions be defined and administered in a politically charged environment? Software is a genuinely "general purpose technology," and if anything, the boundaries defining what is and what is not a *software invention* are likely to become more blurry in the near future, further complicating efforts at developing regimes of intellectual property protection specific to software.

The issue of software patent quality remains an important one, although evidence of sharp declines in the quality of recent patents in this field, assertions to the contrary notwithstanding, remains scarce. Nevertheless, the problem of patent quality in the U.S. system is by no means unique to software but is common in many areas of new inventive activity. The relatively weak administrative procedures in the United States for ensuring patent quality (or enabling administrative challenges by other interested private parties to patents' validity) produce greater uncertainty over patent validity, and the available mechanisms (litigation) almost certainly result in higher costs overall for the resolution of such disputes. Rather than pursuing *sui generis* solutions to the challenges of patenting in software, a broader effort to strengthen administrative procedures for strengthening patent quality seems highly desirable.

Notes

1. R. Mazzoleni and R. R. Nelson, "Economic Theories about the Benefits and Costs of Patents," *Journal of Economic Issues* 32 (1998): 1031–52.

2. E. Mansfield, "Patents and Innovation: An Empirical Study," *Management Science* 32, no. 2 (1986): 173–81; R. C. Levin, A. K. Klevorick, R. R. Nelson, and S. Winter, "Appropriating the Returns to Industrial R & D," *Brookings Papers on Economic Activity* (1987): 783–821; W. Cohen, R. R. Nelson, and J. Walsh, "Protecting Their Intellectual Assets: Appropriability Conditions and Why U.S. Manufacturing Firms Patent (or Not)" (National Bureau of Economic Research working paper 7552, February 2000).

3. See D. C. Mowery, R. R. Nelson, B. N. Sampat, and A. A. Ziedonis, *Ivory Tower and Industrial Innovation: University-Industry Technology Transfer before and after Bayh-Dole* (Stanford, Calif.: Stanford University Press, 2004) for a review of the Bayh-Dole Act's origins and effects.

4. R. P. Merges and R. R. Nelson. "On the Complex Economics of Patent Scope," *Columbia Law Review* 90 (1990): 813–916.

5. S. Scotchmer and J. Green, "Novelty and Disclosure in Patent Law," *RAND Journal of Economics* 21 (1990): 131–46.

6. T. Bresnahan and S. Greenstein, "The Competitive Crash in Large Scale Commercial Computing," in *The Mosaic of Economic Growth*, ed. R. Landau, T. Taylor, and G. Wright (Stanford, Calif.: Stanford University Press, 1996). Bresnahan and Greenstein point out that a similar erosion of multiproduct economies of scope appears to have occurred among computer hardware manufacturers with the introduction of the microcomputer.

7. See D. C. Mowery and T. Simcoe, "The Origins and Evolution of the Internet," in *Technological Innovation and National Economic Performance*, ed. B. Steil, R. Nelson, and D. Victor (Princeton, N.J.: Princeton University Press, 2002).

8. See J. Kuan, "Understanding Open Source Software: A Nonprofit Competitive Threat" (unpublished ms., Haas School of Business, University of California at Berkeley, 1999); J. Lerner and J. Tirole, "The Simple Economics of Open Source" (unpublished ms., Harvard Business School, 2000).

9. A trade secret formally is some information used in a business that, when secret, gives one an advantage over competitors. The secret must be both novel and valuable. *Metallurgical Industries, Inc. v. Fourtek, Inc.* 790 F.2d 1195 (1986).

10. Collectors of valuable information can prevent competitors from using the information. *International News Service v. Associated Press*, 248 U.S. 215 (1911).

11. A trademark protects names, words, and symbols used to identify or distinguish goods and to identify the producer. *Zatrains, Inc. v. Oak Grove Smokehouse, Inc.* 698 F.2d 786 (5th Cir. 1983).

12. Protection is available for software embodied in semiconductor chips, so-called mask works. *E. F. Johnson v. Uniden Corp. of America*, 653 F. Supp. 1485 (D. Minn. 1985).

13. P. Menell, "An Analysis of the Scope of Copyright Protection for Application Programs," *Stanford Law Review* 41 (1989): 1045–96.

14. National Commission on New Technological Uses of Copyrighted Works (CONTU), *Final Report* (Washington, D.C.: U.S. Government Printing Office, 1979).

15. 17 U.S.C. sec. 101, sec. 117 (as amended 1980). For a more complete discussion, see Menell, "Analysis of the Scope." Cited in note 13.

16. 714 F.2d 1240 (3d Cir. 1983). Consistent with its position as a leading firm in the packaged software industry, Microsoft, which supported stronger formal protection for software-related intellectual property, filed an *amicus curiae* brief on behalf of Apple in this case.

17. Historically, a major distinction in the copyright law has been that ideas are not protected, only expressions. *Baker v. Selden*, 101 U.S. 99 (1879).

18. *Computer Associates Int'l v. Altai, Inc.*, 982 F.2d 693 (2d Cir. 1992); *Whelan Associates v. Jaslow Dental Laboratory*, 797 F.2d 1222 (3d Cir. 1986).

19. 450 U.S. 175 (1981).

20. 450 U.S. 381 (1981).

21. R. P. Merges, "A Comparative Look at Intellectual Property Rights and the Software Industry," in *The International Computer Software Industry: A Comparative Study of Industry Evolution and Structure*, ed. D. C. Mowery (New York: Oxford University Press, 1996).

22. Ibid.

23. J. Peltz, "Compton's Wins Patent Covering Multimedia," *Los Angeles Times*, November 16, 1993, D2. The Compton's patent was titled "Multimedia Search Systems Using a Plurality of Entry Path Means Which Indicate Interrelatedness of Information." J. Markoff, "Patent Office to Review a Controversial Award," *New York Times*, December 17, 1993, D2.

24. Abstract, U.S. Patent Number 5,241,671, August 31, 1993.

25. T. Abate, "Smaller, Faster, Better; Tech Firms Show Off Their Latest Wonders at Trade Show and Foretell a User-Friendly Future," *San Francisco Examiner*, November 21, 1993, E1.

26. Markoff, "Patent Office to Review Controversial Award." Cited in note 23.

27. T. Riordan, "Action Was Preliminary on a Disputed Patent," *New York Times*, March 30, 1994, D7.

28. S. Orenstein, "U.S. Rejects Multimedia Patent," *Recorder*, November 1, 1994, 4. For a subsequent history of the reexamination of this patent, see note 1 on page 126 in this volume.

29. 149 F.3d 1368 (CAFC, 1998).

30. "Now we're dealing with a much broader universe of 'prior art,'" says J. T. Westermeier, a Washington, D.C., Internet attorney with Piper and Marbury, pointing out that many allegedly novel Internet business methods may already have been

in use at universities or elsewhere. P. Waldmeir and L. Kehoe, "E-commerce Companies Sue to Protect Patents: Intellectual Rights Given Legal Test," *Financial Times*, October 25, 1999, 16.

31. See http://www.uspto.gov/web/menu/pbmethod/fy2001strport.html. According to the USPTO "Cassis" database, 449 and 423 patents were issued in Class 705, respectively, for 2002 and 2003.

32. An Internet vendor of books and other products, Amazon.com, filed suit in 1999 against Barnes & Noble over the latter's alleged infringement of its patent on "one click" order methods. Although Amazon was granted an injunction against Barnes & Noble's alleged infringement of its "one-click" patent by the District Court for the Western District of Washington State in December 1999, the Court of Appeals reversed the judge in February 2001 and remanded the case to the district court. Given the CAFC's central role in establishing the patentability of business methods, its reversal of an injunction in this case is noteworthy.

33. R. Hart, P. Holmes, and J. Reid, *The Economic Impact of Patentability of Computer Programs: A Report to the European Commission* (London: Intellectual Property Institute, 1999).

34. S. J. H. Graham and D. C. Mowery, "Intellectual Property Protection in the U.S. Software Industry," in *The Patent System in the Knowledge-Based Economy*, ed. W. Cohen and S. Merrill (Washington, D.C.: National Academies Press, 2003).

35. J. Bessen and R. M. Hunt, "An Empirical Look at Software Patents" (unpublished manuscript, Boston University School of Law, 2004).

36. As reported in *Softletter*, "The 2001 Softletter 100," *Softletter Trends and Strategies in Software Publishing* 16 (2001), this group includes Microsoft, Novell, Adobe Systems, Autodesk, Intuit, and Symantec. We chose to focus our analysis on the patents assigned to specialized, publicly traded software firms, because we wanted to use R & D spending figures to compute a software-patent-propensity measure (software patents deflated by R & D spending): This measure is meaningful only for firms reporting R & D spending for which one can assume that the bulk of this R & D spending is devoted to software development, thus precluding many more generalized electronics firms (although these latter firms are engaged in a substantial amount of "software" patenting).

37. We are grateful to *Softletter* for permission to use these data. The 2001 tabulation was the last year to date in which *Softletter* produced this report.

38. "National Software Strategy for Scotland," Scottish Enterprise and the Scottish Software Federation, 2001, www.electrum.co.uk/wwword/nssdoc.html

39. The only class that did not show a reasonably flat growth trajectory after 1998 was the IPC group G06F 17, which is the newest "software" class and showed steady growth as a share of all patenting in 1995–2003.

40. Graham and Mowery, "Intellectual Property Protection." Cited in note 34.

41. Pendency for software applications at issue for all software patents compared to all nonsoftware patents from 1995 to 2003 is as follows:

Year	1995	1996	1997	1998	1999	2000	2001	2002	2003
Pendency	130%	127%	122%	120%	122%	128%	136%	145%	146%

Source: Authors' data analysis of issued U.S. patents.

42. Bessen and Hunt, "Empirical Look at Software Patents." Cited in note 35.

43. Data analysis using the IPC-definition method found substantially the same trend in these firms' patenting shares.

44. This analysis covers only the 1987–2002 period because corporate R & D investment data for 2003 were not available for all of the *Softletter* firms.

45. All patent propensity calculations use constant-dollar firm R & D spending (1987 = $1).

46. R & D spending declined during 2000–2001 in several large firms (Novell, Adobe Systems) as well as in smaller firms (Phoenix Technologies, Macromedia).

47. Intuit is not included in this chart even though it is the fourth largest firm in the 2001 *Softletter* rankings. Because Intuit holds virtually no patents, Autodesk, the fifth largest firm, was included in its stead.

48. We include here two caveats given in Graham and Mowery, "Intellectual Property Protection," cited in note 34, concerning the risks of comparing these two firms' patent propensity: The R & D data reported by these two firms may not be strictly comparable, since a portion of Microsoft's total reported R & D investment may cover some fixed costs of maintaining an R & D facility that are not included in IBM's reported software-related R & D investment (although IBM does maintain "software only" research facilities around the globe; its Bangalore, India, LINUX facilities are but one example). In addition, an unknown portion of Microsoft's reported R & D spending includes development programs for hardware—these data therefore may understate the Microsoft software-related patent propensity and overstate that for IBM.

49. Ibid.

50. S. D. Hunter, "Have Business Methods Patents Gotten a Bum Rap? Some Empirical Evidence" (working paper no. 4326-03, Sloan School, MIT, 2003).

51. Menell, "Analysis of the Scope of Copyright Protection," 1047. Cited in note 13.

52. See also R. P. Merges, "As Many as Six Impossible Patents before Breakfast: Property Rights for Business Concepts and Patent System Reform," *Berkeley Technology Law Journal* 14 (1999): 577–615.

53. B. H. Hall, S. J. H. Graham, D. Harhoff, and D. C. Mowery, "Prospects for Improving U.S. Patent Quality via Post-Grant Opposition," in *Innovation Policy and the Economy*, vol. 4, ed. A. Jaffe, J. Lerner, and S. Stern (Cambridge, Mass.: MIT Press for NBER, 2004).

54. See J. Bessen and E. Maskin, "Sequential Innovation, Patents, and Innovation" (working paper, Economics Department, MIT, 2000); Bessen and Hunt, "Empirical Look at Software Patents." Cited in note 35.

55. B. H. Hall, "Business Method Patents and Innovation" (paper presented at the Atlanta Federal Reserve Bank Conference on Business Method Patents, Sea Island, Ga., April 3–5, 2003), 10.

56. B. H. Hall and R. H. Ziedonis, "The Patent Paradox Revisited: Determinants of Patenting in the US Semiconductor Industry, 1980–1994," *RAND Journal of Economics* 32, no. 1 (2001): 101–28.

57. R. A. Guth and D. Clark, "Behind Secret Settlement Talks: New Power of Tech Customers," *Wall Street Journal*, April 5, 2004, 1.

58. S. J. Graham, "Continuation, Complementarity, and Capturing Value: Three Studies Exploring Firms' Complementary Uses of Appropriability Mechanisms in Technological Innovation" (PhD diss., Haas School of Business, University of California at Berkeley, 2004).

59. See, for example, Bessen and Hunt, "Empirical Look at Software Patents." Cited in note 35.

60. Ibid.

4

Designing Optimal Software Patents

Dan L. Burk and Mark A. Lemley

Over the past three decades, U.S. patent law has come to fully embrace the patentability of computer software, an acceptance that is at least arguably desirable and almost certainly irreversible. Software is at core a utilitarian artifact, better suited to the protective mechanisms of patent than those of the alternative copyright.[1] As a practical matter, the software industry has long sought the inclusion of software within patentable subject matter and seems unlikely to surrender now that the goal has been achieved. Finally, although a few nations have fought a desperate rearguard action against software patenting, it has rapidly become the international standard, further consolidating the software patent norm.

In this chapter, we accept as given the proposition that patent law has a positive role to play in fostering software innovation, but argue that this will not occur as the state of software patenting currently stands. We suggest that the present contours of software patenting are poorly tailored to the realities of the industry, and require adjustment in order to foster software innovation. We begin by reviewing the current state of patent law vis-à-vis software, focusing on the patentability requirements of obviousness and disclosure. We describe in particular how the United States Court of Appeals for the Federal Circuit (CAFC), the court charged with jurisdiction for the matters of patent law, has developed a highly permissive disclosure standard for software, but a potentially restrictive obviousness standard. We then review the innovation profile of the software industry, noting its relatively low development costs, short product cycles, incremental development, and reliance on reverse engineering. These characteristics, we argue, are poorly matched to the current scope and availability of software patents as developed elaborated by the CAFC. We conclude with certain suggestions as to how the contours of the software patents could be better fitted to the innovation needs of the software industry.

Software Patents

Software is presently well understood to be patentable subject matter, although this understanding is the result of a long and tortured history of doctrinal development.[2] For many years, the United States Court of Appeals for the Federal Circuit moved by fits and starts toward declaring software patentable. Finally, with the late-1990s decisions in *State Street Bank*[3] and *AT&T v. Excel*,[4] the court unreservedly admitted software to the canon of patentable subject matter. In doing so, the court emphasized that it was deciding only the question of subject matter: whether software is the sort of invention that can be patented.[5] For any given software invention, the remaining statutory criteria for patentability must be worked out on a case-by-case basis.[6] These criteria include the requirement that the invention be novel,[7] that is, not previously known; that the invention be nonobvious,[8] that is, that it be a significant technological advance; and that it comply with statutory disclosure requirements.[9] These patentability criteria must be met for all types of inventions. But the subsequent development of cases concerning these requirements has generated a unique and technology-specific set of criteria for software.

Disclosure. Section 112 of the U.S. Patent Act requires that patentees publish to the world a description of the invention sufficient to enable one of ordinary skill in the art to make and use it, as well as setting forth the "best mode" of implementing the invention.[10] These requirements of enablement, description, and "best mode" are fundamental prerequisites for obtaining a patent. Indeed, this disclosure requirement is central to the patent policy "bargain" between patentees and the public; the public grants patent rights on condition of invention disclosure.[11] Disclosure serves the public interest in two ways. First, disclosure enables competitors to make use of the patented invention once the patent expires, adding to the available knowledge in the art and ensuring that the invention ultimately enters the public domain.[12] Second, during the term of the patent itself, disclosure enables others to improve on the patented technology, either by "designing around" the patent to produce a noninfringing variant[13] or by developing a better version that, while infringing, is itself entitled to its own improvement patent.[14]

For software patents, however, a series of recent Federal Circuit decisions has drastically curtailed the enablement and best mode requirements. In recent years, the CAFC has held that software patentees need not disclose source or object code, flowcharts, or detailed descriptions of the patented program. Rather, the court has found high-level functional description sufficient to satisfy both the enablement and best mode doctrines.[15] For example, in *Northern Telecom, Inc. v. Datapoint Corp.*,[16] the patent claimed an improved method of entering, verifying, and storing (or "batching") data with a special data entry terminal. The district court invalidated certain claims of the patent on the grounds that they were inadequately disclosed under section 112. The CAFC reversed. It held that, when claims pertain to a computer program that implements a claimed device or method, the enablement requirement varies according to the nature of the claimed invention as well as the role and complexity of the computer program needed to implement it. The court reasoned that, under the facts in this case, the core of the claimed invention was the combination of components or steps, rather than the details of the program the applicant actually used.

The court in *Northern Telecom* noted expert testimony to the effect that various programs could be used to implement the invention, and that it would be "relatively straightforward [in light of the specification] for a skilled computer programmer to design a program to carry out the claimed invention."[17] Indeed, the court continued to state that the expression of a desired function into programming language is "a mere clerical function to a skilled programmer."[18] Similarly, in *Fonar Corp. v. General Electric Co.*,[19] discussing the patentee's obligation to disclose the best mode of practicing an invention, the Court explained that descriptions of software are "satisfied by a disclosure of the functions of the software" because "writing code for such software is within the skill of the art" once functions are disclosed. Thus, there is no need to disclose source code or detailed flow charts, only function.[20]

Indeed, in a few cases the CAFC has gone so far as to hold that patentees can satisfy the written description and best mode requirements for inventions implemented in software even though they do not use the terms *computer* or *software* anywhere in the specification of the invention![21] To be sure, in these latter cases, it would probably be obvious to one skilled in the art that the particular feature in question should be implemented in software. And one recent case moves in the other direction, holding that an oil drilling company failed to enable its method for calculating the location of a borehole when it kept all information about the computer programs used to perform the calculation secret.[22] Still, it is remarkable that the CAFC is willing to find the enablement requirement satisfied by a patent specification that provides *no* guidance whatsoever on how the software should be written.[23]

Programming is a highly technical and difficult art. It is simply unrealistic to think that one of ordinary skill in the programming field can necessarily reconstruct a computer program given no more than the purpose the program is to perform. But the CAFC's peculiar direction in the software enablement cases has effectively nullified the disclosure obligation in those cases. And, since source code is normally kept secret, software patentees generally disclose little or no detail about their programs in the patent. Software patentees during the 1980s and early 1990s tended to write their patents in means-plus-function format[24] in order to satisfy the changing dictates of the CAFC's patentable subject matter rules.[25] Lawyers writing patents in such a format have an incentive to describe their invention in the specification in as general terms as possible, since means-plus-function claim elements will be limited to the actual structure disclosed in the specification and equivalents thereof.[26] As a result, there is no easy way to figure out what a software patent owner has built except to reverse engineer the program.[27]

Obviousness. The disclosure requirement as applied to software has created a discrete body of precedent unique to that technology. But the court's reasoning in the enablement and best mode cases has another implication as well. Because the court views actually writing and debugging a program as a "mere clerical function" "within the skill of the art," it follows that the court is unlikely to consider the work of programming itself to be sufficiently innovative to meet the nonobviousness threshold of section 103.

This is because patent law uses much the same test for gauging obviousness as for gauging adequacy of disclosure; in each case, the question of whether one of ordinary skill in the art is able to make the patented invention without undue experimentation is central to the inquiry.[28]

While only a limited number of appellate decisions discuss obviousness in the context of software patents, there is some reason to believe the court is imposing a rather strict standard. The first case involving the obviousness of a software-implemented invention is, perhaps surprisingly, a Supreme Court case from the 1970s. In *Dann v. Johnston*,[29] the Court held a patent on a "machine system for automatic record-keeping of bank checks and deposits" invalid for obviousness. The Court took a rather broad view of obviousness in the computer industry, focusing on whether systems analogous to the patentee's had been implemented in computers before, rather than analyzing the precise differences between the patentee's program and the prior art programs. The clear implication of the opinion is that if a reasonably skilled programmer could produce a program analogous to the patented one, and if there was motivation in the prior art to do so, the patented program is obvious.

The Federal Circuit has found software patents invalid for obviousness in two recent cases, *Lockwood v. American Airlines*[30] and *Amazon.com v. Barnesandnoble.com. Inc.*[31] Neither case opined directly on the ease with which computer programs could be produced, but both viewed obviousness as a rather substantial hurdle to patentability of software.[32] In *Lockwood*, the question was whether the defendant's own system made the patented claims obvious. The system had been in public use, but American Airlines had kept the workings of the system secret. Nonetheless, because Lockwood's patent was claimed in broad functional terms, the court found that similarly broad functional disclosures in the prior art were sufficient to render the patent obvious. While Lockwood argued that the information provided was not sufficient for one skilled in the art to make and use the system, the court pointed out that it was as detailed as the information Lockwood's own patent provided.[33] Thus, the patent's meager disclosure of technical details indirectly contributed to the court's finding of obviousness.

In *Amazon.com*, the court found Amazon's "one-click" shopping feature to be obvious in view of certain references describing the desirability or feasibility of such a system in general terms, and one prior system that delivered data online in response to a mouse click. The court rejected arguments that the one-click feature was technically difficult to implement, relying on the fact that the prior art generally described such a system as both desirable and feasible. The court also gave surprisingly short shrift to Amazon's evidence of secondary considerations of nonobviousness.[34]

The likely result of the CAFC's focus on high-level functionality is that improvements in programming techniques will be found obvious in view of prior art that solved the same basic problem in a somewhat different way. This was arguably the result in both *Dann* and *Lockwood*,[35] and it seems to follow from the court's view in the section 112 cases that programmers are an extremely skilled group of individuals, who can write a given program with little guidance from the patentee. This also implies that for a program to be nonobvious to those of such skill in the art, it will have to be an extremely significant advance over the prior art. While disclosure is a minimal hurdle for software patents then, obviousness can be a rather tough one.

This argument may strike the reader as somewhat surprising. After all, legions of scholars and commentators complain that the U.S. Patent and Trademark Office (USPTO) issues too many software patents, and in particular, it issues patents on subject matter that should be considered obvious.[36] We agree with these commentators that the USPTO is issuing bad software patents, in part because it cannot find relevant prior art.[37] But our point is a different one: Those patents will not fare well in litigation because the CAFC will consider them obvious in view of any other computer program that implements the same basic concepts, regardless of how different those programs are in detailed implementation. Further, while hidden prior art is indeed a problem, parties in litigation have far more time and money to spend than patent examiners, and they are much more likely than the USPTO to find the best prior art. The probable result is that, while numerous software patents will issue, a large number of those actually litigated will be found obvious.

Patent Scope. Patent scope is necessarily interrelated with obviousness and enablement.[38] The breadth of patent protection is in part a function of how different the invention is from the prior art. Further, patent claims are invalid if they are not fully described and enabled by the patent specification, so the permissible breadth of a patent will be determined by how much information the court determines must be disclosed to enable one of ordinary skill in the art to make and use the patented invention. Obviousness and enablement also define patent law's doctrine of equivalents, which states that trivial substitutions in an allegedly infringing device will not place it beyond the scope of the patent, even if the substitutions are not explicitly claimed in the patent. The scope of equivalents covered by a patent is a function of obviousness and enablement, since a patentee is not permitted to capture ground under the doctrine of equivalents that it would not have been permitted to claim in the first place.[39]

The CAFC's treatment of software validity issues suggests that, while the court will find relatively few software patents nonobvious, those that it does approve will be entitled to broad protection. The CAFC's decisions strongly suggest that a patent is nonobvious only if it is the first program to perform a given function. Most software patents will not meet this test, of course, but those that do will not be constrained by prior art to claim only their particular implementation of a function. They can claim the function itself. And the fact that they give little or no description of how to achieve this function will be no bar to the broad claims, because the court has proven remarkably unwilling to require software patentees to disclose details. As a result, we should expect the first to implement a new idea in software to claim the entire category of software, regardless of how second comers actually implement the same concept.

The evidence on software patent claim scope so far is mixed, although there is some evidence tending to support this hypothesis. Most notably, in *Interactive Gift Express v. Compuserve*,[40] the patentee had designed a kiosk system for printing copyrighted works on demand. The CAFC held that the claims of the patent should be read broadly, to cover any form of online downloading in response to a remote request.[41] In doing so, it reversed the district court's construction of five separate claim elements. As construed by the CAFC, the patent is breathtaking in its scope, and most electronic commerce sites that permit downloading of digital information are likely within its ambit.

The court's treatment of software patent scope under the doctrine of equivalents has been even less uniform. Many of these decisions have rejected application of the doctrine of equivalents to read claim language written for one product generation at such a high level of abstraction that it covers accused products from a different generation. Thus, in *Alpex Computer Corp.*

v. Nintendo Co.,[42] the CAFC held that a patent claim to a video game output display system was not infringed by a next-generation system that worked in a different way. Alpex's claimed system included a display RAM that stored information corresponding to each pixel of a television screen in a discrete location. Nintendo's accused device, by contrast, used shift registers to store one "slice" of the video display at any given time. The CAFC rejected a jury finding that the two systems were equivalent.[43] In *Digital Biometrics, Inc. v. Identix, Inc.*,[44] the court construed narrowly a patent claim to "image arrays" storing a two-dimensional slice of video data, which were merged into a "composite array" storing a fingerprint image. The court held that the defendant's systems, which constructed the composite array directly rather than by using two-dimensional slices, did not create "image arrays" within the meaning of the claims. More recently, in *Wang Laboratories, Inc. v. America Online*,[45] the court affirmed a district court decision granting summary judgment of noninfringement under the doctrine of equivalents. The patent claims in that case covered "frames," defined in the specification as pages encoded in character-based protocols. The court rejected Wang's attempt to extend the patent to cover bit-mapped pages, crediting evidence that there were "huge, huge differences" between the two approaches.[46]

Other cases have applied the doctrine of equivalents more broadly. In some of those cases, the CAFC has found equivalence between two different types of software programs written in different product generations. More troubling, some cases suggest that software implementations of certain ideas are equivalent to older mechanical implementations. An example is *Overhead Door Corp. v. Chamberlain Group, Inc.*[47] The patented system claimed a (mechanical) switch connected to a microprocessor that could store the codes of multiple garage doors. The CAFC held that the claim was not literally infringed by an electronic switch implemented in software. However, the court reversed a grant of summary judgment to the defendants under the doctrine of equivalents, concluding that a reasonable jury could find that the difference between mechanical and software implementations was a mere "design choice."

WMS Gaming, Inc. v. International Game Technology[48] is also instructive. In that case, the court held that a claim written in means-plus-function language that relied for its corresponding structure on a computer programmed with a particular algorithm was limited in literal scope to the particular algorithm chosen and equivalents thereof. However, the court found the defendant's algorithm infringing under the doctrine of equivalents, presumably because it was largely indifferent to which algorithm implemented the function of the program. This latter approach has the potential to expand the scope of patents in the software industry dramatically.[49]

Software patents, then, are likely to face serious obviousness hurdles. The few patents that overcome those hurdles need disclose virtually nothing about the detailed workings of their invention and will likely be broadly interpreted to cover a variety of mechanisms for implementing the basic software invention. We would expect the outcome of such a patent policy to be an industry dominated by a relatively small number of broad patents. This configuration of patents may be optimal for certain industries; for example, it fits well the innovation profile for the pharmaceutical industry, where innovation costs are extremely high and product development times extremely protracted. But, as we show in the next section, the software patent criteria developed by the CAFC will lead not only to suboptimal results for software innovation but to a patent distribution that is decidedly detrimental to the industry.

Software Innovation

Patent law is our primary policy tool to promote innovation, encourage the development of new technologies, and increase the fund of human knowledge. Although there exist a variety of theories to explain how patents best accomplish this goal, there is virtually unanimous agreement that the purpose of the patent system is to promote innovation by granting exclusive rights to encourage invention. Industries vary in their innovation profiles, however, and in order to optimally encourage innovation, the scope of rights offered by a patent should match the needs of a given industry. Patents that would be perfectly tailored to the needs of one industry may be too narrow or too broad for another, failing in the first case to stimulate innovation investment, or disastrously stifling innovative activity in the second.

Software is a prime example of an industry with its own peculiar innovation requirements. The computer industry is characterized by a large number of rapid, iterative improvements on existing products.[50] Computer programs normally build on preexisting ideas and often on prior code itself.[51] This incremental improvement is desirable for a variety of reasons. First, it responds to the hardware-based architectural constraints of the software industry. Data storage capacity, processing speed, and transmission rates have all increased steadily over time.[52] Programs written during an older period therefore faced capacity constraints that disappear over time. It makes sense to improve those products progressively as the constraints that limit the functionality of the programs disappear.

Second, incremental improvement of existing programs and ideas tends to render programs more stable. It is received wisdom in the industry that customers should avoid version 1.0 of any software product, because its maker is unlikely to have all the bugs worked out. Iterative programs built on a single base tend to solve these problems over time. This is most obviously true when actual computer code is reused,[53] but it is true even when tested algorithms or structures are replicated in new programs. And as a related matter, iterative improvement helps preserve interoperability, both among generations of the same program and across programs.[54]

The software industry also has relatively low fixed costs and a short time to market. Software inventions tend to have a quick, cheap, and fairly straightforward postinvention development cycle. Most of the work in software development occurs in the initial coding, not in development or production. While the costs of writing software have increased substantially over time as programs have become more complex, the costs of writing and manufacturing computer programs remain low relative to the fixed costs of development in many industries. Debugging and test marketing are tedious and potentially time consuming, but they do not rival the cost of stringent safety testing and agency oversight that are necessary in other innovation sectors such as the biotechnology and pharmaceutical industries.[55]

Furthermore, computer program life cycles are short. The lead time to market in the software industry tends to be brief. Unlike industries such as steel or aircraft, where new generations of products are infrequent and those products may last for decades, computer programs tend to be replaced every few years, and sometimes even yearly, often by new versions of the same program.

More critically, from the perspective of innovation policy, the ratio of innovation cost to the cost of follow-on competition is not particularly high.

While it does cost less to clone someone else's program than to design your own from scratch, the difference is not enormous.[56] This is in part because the capital investment requirement for software development is relatively low, consisting mostly of hiring personnel, not building laboratories or manufacturing infrastructure. The archetypal software invention is one made by two people working in a garage.[57]

Additionally, software development relies heavily on reverse engineering practices to allow either follow-on or compatible product development. Many commentators have explained the importance of permitting competitors to reverse engineer a product to see how it works and discover ways to design around it.[58] Additionally, because software devices must interoperate with other software, reverse engineering is often important to producing compatible, let alone competing, products. Decompilation of a competitor's object code is often an important step in producing new software products; software devices typically cannot be readily understood by casual inspection, and particularly not without access to human-readable source code or other documentation.

Optimal Patent Design

These industry characteristics are precisely those suggested by cumulative innovation theory. The economics of cumulative innovation map very well onto the modern software industry. The theory of cumulative innovation starts by rejecting the proposition that invention is an activity engaged in by a single inventor or company acting in isolation. Rather, cumulative innovation is an ongoing, iterative process that requires the contributions of many different inventors, each building on the work of others.[59] Cumulative innovation theory questions the ability of any one inventor to identify and coordinate all the improvers needed to optimize a product over time. Instead, economists who emphasize cumulative innovation argue that the law must divide property entitlements to provide incentives to each improver in the process. The implications of these economic characteristics for patent law are threefold. First, the need for strong patent protection is somewhat less for software inventions than it is in other industries. Unlike paradigmatic patent-dependent industries such as biotechnology and chemical manufacturing, where broad patent protection is critical due to high innovation cost and an uncertain development process, software development presents a relatively low-cost innovation profile. Software patents are important, but the relatively low fixed costs associated with software development, coupled with other forms of overlapping intellectual property protection for software,[60] mean that innovation in software does not depend critically on strong, broad protection.

Second, the rapid, incremental innovation crucial to the software industry may be retarded by older companies that own software patents based on prior generations of products. The danger is that a single patent covers not just a single product, but several generations of products that reflect incremental improvements by a number of different companies. Cohen and Lemley offer several reasons to fear that the doctrine of equivalents may be applied too broadly in the software industry, allowing owners of old software patents to prevent the development of new generations of technology.[61] It is worth noting, however, that the CAFC decisions on this point are decidedly mixed.[62]

Finally, a culture of rapid-fire incremental improvements leads to a large number of low-level innovations. Copyright is incapable of providing effective protection for such innovations because it does not protect functionality.[63] Some form of protection for such innovations is desirable. Because innovation is relatively low cost but rapid, the need for patent protection is generally modest. Patent protection for such incremental software inventions should be relatively easy to acquire, but it should be narrow. In particular, software patents should not generally extend across several product generations.[64] In the absence of other forms of protection, a large number of narrow software patents may be the best way of protecting these low-level innovations.[65]

The question then is how to adjust current patent law to achieve this outcome of narrower and more-abundant patents. The patent statute itself provides the necessary tools. More than a decade ago, Robert Merges suggested that the nonobviousness doctrine should be adjusted commensurate with the costs of innovation in a given industry.[66] The higher the cost to bring an invention to market, the bigger the potential reward should be, in order to attract the necessary investment. Bigger potential rewards can be provided by increasing the likelihood of obtaining a patent, and the likelihood of obtaining a patent can be increased by lowering the obvious-ness barrier. Conversely, the obviousness barrier should be heightened where the cost of innovation is lower and the need for a patent incentive is less.

Because innovation in software is relatively less uncertain than in indus-tries like biotechnology, Merges's economic framework suggests that the nonobviousness bar should be rather high.[67] A few broad software patents are indeed what the current CAFC jurisprudence will likely produce. By relaxing the enablement requirement and permitting software inventions to be defined in broad terms, supported by very little in the way of detailed disclosure, the CAFC has encouraged software patents to be drafted broadly and applied to allegedly infringing devices that are far removed from the original patented invention. By implication, the CAFC's standard also seems to suggest that many narrower software patents on low-level incremental improvements will be invalid for obviousness in view of earlier, more gen-eral disclosures. They may also be invalidated under the on-sale bar, because the Supreme Court's view that a software invention is "ready for patenting"[68] when it is the subject of a commercial order and when the inventor has described its broad functions, even if it is not clear how the code will be written or that it will work for its intended purpose,[69] means that any patentee who waits until the code is written to file a patent appli-cation risks being time-barred for not filing earlier.

Unfortunately, when matched up against actual industry needs, the CAFC's current standard seems to be precisely backward. Software is an industry characterized, at least to a limited extent, by competition theory[70] and, to a greater extent, by cumulative innovation. Cumulative innovation theory suggests that patent protection for incremental software inventions should be relatively easy to acquire in order to reward incremental improve-ments, implying a somewhat lower obviousness threshold. It also suggests that the resulting patents should be narrow and, in particular, that they should not generally extend across several product generations for fear of stifling subsequent incremental improvements. This in turn means that software patents should be limited in scope.[71]

Implementing a rational software policy obviously requires some sig-nificant changes to existing case law. A number of patentability doctrines might be brought to bear on this problem. First, obviousness doctrine needs to be reformed, preferably by way of a more informed application of the level of skill in the art[72] or, alternatively, by application of new secondary considerations of nonobviousness.[73] Second, a higher disclosure requirement and restrictions on the doctrine of equivalents will help reduce patent scope.[74]

Additionally, the reverse engineering needs of the software industry are not accommodated under current patent law. In the case of copyright, courts have adapted the doctrine of fair use, sometimes together with copyright misuse, to allow competitors to engage in reverse engineering of computer software.[75] Patent law, however, includes no express provision allowing reverse engineering, nor is there any judicially developed exception akin to copyright's fair use doctrine that might permit it. Indeed, patent law generally lacks provisions akin to fair use or other exceptions that might readily be pressed into the service of reverse engineering, although commentators have suggested that patent law may need such exceptions for precisely this reason.[76]

This does not mean that reverse engineering a patented product is necessarily illegal under patent law. Some inventions, such as the paper clip, are readily apparent once embodied in a product.[77] Improvers do not need to reverse engineer the paper clip to determine how it works in order to improve it; they just need to look at it. Additionally, in many cases, the patentee has done all the work necessary for reverse engineering patented inventions by disclosing how to make and use the claimed invention in the patent specification. In theory, an express provision authorizing reverse engineering would be superfluous if the enabling disclosures required to secure a patent were sufficiently strong: Someone who wanted to learn how a patented device worked would need only to read the patent specification.[78]

Patentable inventions in software, however, generally do not have these characteristics.[79] Examination of the patent itself is unlikely to yield information equivalent to a reverse engineered inspection because the CAFC does not require would-be patentees of software inventions to disclose the implementing source code or, for that matter, very much at all about their inventions.[80] Accordingly, software patents present unique obstacles to consummation of the patent law's traditional rights-for-disclosure bargain with the public.

The specific reverse engineering techniques commonly used for software, in turn, may raise some infringement problems that are unique to software. The definition of infringement in the patent statute is extremely broad, encompassing anyone who "makes, uses, offers to sell, . . . sells . . . , or imports" a patented product.[81] Reverse engineering a patented computer program by decompiling[82] it likely fits within this broad category of prohibited conduct, at least where the program itself is claimed as an apparatus. Reverse engineering clearly constitutes a "use" of the patented software, although owners of a particular copy of the program surely have the right to use it.[83] More significantly, decompilation may also constitute "making" the patented program by generating a temporary yet functional copy of it in RAM memory[84] and, in certain instances, a longer-term (though still "intermediate") copy in more permanent memory. Thus, an article-of-manufacture claim to a particular program "encoded on a computer hard drive" might be infringed by a reverse engineered copy temporarily stored on a computer hard drive. Those copies probably constitute patent infringement unless protected by some defense. The result of all of this is that the nominally neutral patent law rule—no defense for reverse engineering—affects software more than other industries.

The need for a reverse engineering exception in patent law militates in favor of adapting the existing doctrines of exhaustion or experimental use to that end.[85] Patent misuse might also be adapted, as it has been in the copyright arena, to prevent patent holders from deterring or prohibiting reverse engineering related to their inventions. The exception might even be created by reinterpreting the infringement provisions of Section 271(a). The resulting patent doctrine would constitute a macro policy lever. As Cohen and Lemley observe, in most industries there is either no need to reverse engineer an invention or reverse engineering can be done without infringing the patent.[86] Only in software is there a need for a particular doctrine to protect the right to reverse engineer, and therefore the ability of improvers to innovate. Thus, a judicially created reverse engineering defense would make sense across the board in software cases but not in other patent cases.

Institutional Competence

This tailoring of patent law to accommodate the innovation profile of software requires the active interpretation and reinterpretation of flexible standards embedded in the patent statute. We believe that the patent statute is properly designed to facilitate precisely such interpretive activity and that courts both can and should use their common-law rulemaking discretion to engage in deliberate, industry-specific modulation of the statute.[87] The business of innovation is too dynamic for the patent system to function successfully in any other way. Not only do new technologies come into existence and old technologies fade into obscurity, but the innovation profile of industries varies from sector to sector and from time to time. Broad disparities exist across economic sectors in the cost of research and development, the length of product cycles, the return on investment, and the cost of obtaining patents itself. The incentives necessary to promote innovation in the pharmaceutical industry are not those necessary to software or to semiconductors. The incentives necessary to a mature software industry are not those that were once necessary to nascent software developers.

Legislative Competence. Only a dynamically interpreted statute can hope to meet the needs of so many disparate industries. The likelihood that a unitary, unvarying, and monolithic statute could supply the correct level of incentive under so many circumstances is essentially nil. The prospect for the legislature to continually revisit the circumstances of each industry and pass appropriate new legislation for each situation is equally untenable; as Grant Gilmore long ago observed, "[G]etting a statute enacted in the first place is much easier than getting the statute revised so that it will make sense in the light of changed conditions."[88] In democratically elected legislatures, an enormous commitment of political capital is typically required to draft, promulgate, and reach consensus on new intellectual property legislation, especially if the legislation is to be supported by credible fact-finding and reliable expertise. The issues involved here are typically not magnets of populist sentiment, and are more likely to be viewed as esoteric and obscure to voters. We can anticipate serious legislative investigation of, and response to, specialized industry needs to be relatively rare events.

But past experience with such specialized statutes is not encouraging. In the United States, the poster child for failed *sui generis* legislation has been the notoriously neglected Semiconductor Chip Protection Act (SCPA). Passed at the behest of the U.S. semiconductor industry after six years of legislative debate, the SCPA created a detailed set of rules designed to protect the "mask work" or circuit design pattern etched into semiconductor chips. The statute was tailored specifically to the purported needs of the industry, including special provisions on reverse engineering and other practices common to semiconductor circuit design. The ostensible reason was to protect American innovation from foreign competitors. But the statute has virtually never been used to enforce the rights it created, generating only one published judicial opinion since its enactment.[89] The most likely reason is that the particular focus of the SCPA—duplication of mask works—is obsolete because the nature of the semiconductor business changed to make the manufacturing process much more difficult, hence harder to imitate at low cost.[90] The foreign competition so feared by U.S. chip fabricators has all but vanished, and the industry appears to be thriving without recourse to its specialized statute.

A similar story could be told regarding industry-specific patent statutes, such as the biotechnology-specific amendments to the U.S. patent statute's obviousness provisions.[91] Like the SCPA, the biotechnology obviousness provisions were enacted after lobbying by the biotechnology industry, which claimed that the general standard for obviousness failed to meet the special process-based characteristics of their industry, requiring a *sui generis* standard. But the biotechnology amendment became irrelevant nearly as soon as it was enacted, in part because general patent standards now reach the same result,[92] and lack the more onerous procedural requirements of the specialized provision.

Preliminary studies of the U.S. Plant Patent Act and Plant Variety Protection Act, as well as the European Union's relatively recent database directive, suggest that similar stories might be told in the case of those specialty statutes as well.[93] The sorry history of such industry-specific statutes suggests that they typically turn out to be failures, because they are drafted with the technology at the time of their passage in mind and are not sufficiently general to accommodate the inevitable changes in technology. This general problem with statutory obsolescence was identified by Guido Calabresi more than twenty years ago,[94] and becomes particularly acute in the case of technologically oriented statutes.[95] Indeed, the likely disinterest of the general populace in such legislative amendments lends itself to a corollary and more serious concern as predicted both by public choice theory and by practical experience.[96] Each time the legislature reopens the patent statute to amendment, the opportunity arises for counterproductive lobbying by special interest groups, not the least of which will be the industry to which the amendment is directed. Technology-specific patent legislation encourages rent-seeking, either by those who stand to benefit directly from favorable legislation or by those who will seize each new legislative opportunity to hijack the amendment process for their own benefit. This has been the history of the U.S. copyright statute, where industry-specific rules and exceptions have led to a bloated, impenetrable statute that reads like the tax code, which is itself the product of such special-interest rent-seeking.[97] Patent law has some balance today in part because different industries have different interests, making it difficult for any one interest group to push through changes to the statute. Industry-specific legislation is much more vulnerable to industry capture. It is no accident that the industry-specific portions of the patent law are among the most complex and confusing sections,[98] and have had some pernicious consequences.[99]

Judicial Competence. These shortcomings in the legislative process militate in favor of judicial oversight for industry-specific tailoring of innovation incentives. This viewpoint stands admittedly at odds with the conventional view that legislatures carry an inherent institutional advantage in detailed fact-finding, and in reflecting social consensus. However, statutes exist on a continuum. At one end lie the kind of tightly drafted detailed rules, such as the U.S. tax code, that Grant Gilmore characterized as "aimed at an unearthly and superhuman precision."[100] As Gilmore noted, such statutes are drafted precisely to curtail judicial interpretation but are nearly impossible to adjust "to changing conditions without legislative revision."[101]

At the other end of the continuum lie general delegations of authority to judges to make correct decisions.[102] The U.S. Sherman Act presents a good example of such a statute, where a set of relatively short directions has generated a robust body of antitrust law. While the statute sets the basic parameters for patentability and infringement, it does not specify in any detail how those basic principles are to be applied. And, in many instances, judicially created doctrines have played a major role in defining the scope of patent protection.[103] Such tailoring activity necessarily vests a fair degree of discretion in the judiciary in order to adapt the general statute to the particular circumstance.

As a general principle, a flexible approach, favoring ongoing judicial oversight, best accommodates new and different technologies within the general framework of a patent statute. Skeptics about the relative merits of judicial oversight may with some justification object that litigation is not cost free and that the courts, appellate courts in particular, are not entirely immune from problems of public choice. However, all advantages are comparative, and the question is not whether courts are the perfect policy tailors, but whether, given the evils of industry-specific statutes here described, courts are better situated to engage in tailoring than the legislature. Court-based tailoring occurs within a particular context, whereby litigation costs purchase not only resolution of a private dispute but the public good of judicial decision making; the costs of dispute resolution in effect subsidize statutory upkeep. Within this context, courts have substantial ability to profile an industry and adapt competition policy according to the profile, within a reasonable time frame and at reasonable cost. Courts are routinely expected to fill this function in areas such as antitrust. Common-law courts can fulfill a similar role in patent law and have indeed done so with regard to a variety of other patentability criteria.

Agency Competence. Courts and legislatures, of course, are not the only institutions available to address statutory upkeep; administrative agencies constitute a third option. There is an argument sometimes made that agencies offer the best of both institutional worlds, having greater expertise and investigatory resources than courts, without the special-interest rent-seeking of legislatures. But, in reality, it is probably necessary to recognize that the middle road of administrative agencies to some extent partakes of the worst of both worlds.[104] Administrative agencies are by no means independent from the legislative forces of public choice, and the same legislator who succumbs to the pressure of special interest groups likely controls the budget of the agency that deals with those groups.[105] But, at the same time, neither is the staff of the administrative agency directly accountable to voters, removing even the threat that voters might overcome collective action problems to impose discipline on imprudent or improper actions. Additionally, the problem of direct capture may be greatly exacerbated in this context. To the extent that an administrative agency interacts repeatedly with a particular constituency, especially a constituency with whom it shares particular expertise, that constituency is likely to exercise undue influence on the agency's rule-making process.

This is not to say that an agency, in this particular case the Patent Office, cannot play a carefully modulated adjunct role in statutory upkeep. Most particularly, there may be such a role if the agency can be held to what it does best, which is fact-finding, without becoming involved in setting legal standards, which is the strong suit of the courts. In this regard, it is important to note that the Supreme Court has extended to the Patent Office a standard of review that grants it judicial deference in fact-finding, without (so far) granting deference in statutory interpretation.[106] This may be in part intended to temper the discretion vested in the specialized patent jurisdiction of the United States Court of Appeals for the Federal Circuit.[107] Nonetheless, even allowing for a fact-finding role on the part of the Patent Office, the modulation of legal standards for particular industries remains in the hands of the courts, and the courts remain the best institutional choice available for that particular role.

Conclusion

Current doctrinal approaches to software patenting have been characterized by high obviousness barriers and low disclosure barriers, a recipe for generating a few dominant patents of broad scope. But this is precisely the wrong outcome for an industry characterized by rapid, cumulative, and incremental innovation. By adjusting the doctrines of obviousness and disclosure to allow narrower but more frequent patenting, as well as by invoking experimental use and related doctrines to permit reverse engineering, courts can tailor the patent system to better serve the innovation needs of software production.

Notes

1. Copyright is designed to protect aesthetic rather than functional creations and in fact excludes functional or utilitarian works from its scope. See Dan L. Burk, "Patenting Speech," *Texas Law Review* 79 (2000): 100.

2. See, e.g., Julie E. Cohen and Mark A. Lemley, "Patent Scope and Innovation in the Software Industry," *California Law Review* 89 (2001): 1; Pamela Samuelson, "Benson Revisited: The Case against Patent Protection for Algorithms and Other Computer Program-Related Inventions," *Emory Law Journal* 39 (1990): 1025, 1033, n. 24.

3. *State Street Bank & Trust Co. v. Signature Financial Group, Inc.,* 149 F.3d 1368 (Fed. Cir. 1998).

4. *AT&T Corp. v. Excel Communications, Inc.,* 172 F.3d 1352 (Fed. Cir. 1999).

5. 35 U.S.C. §101.

6. See *State Street*, 149 F.3d at 1375. Indeed, on remand in *AT&T*, the district court held the patent invalid under section 102. *AT&T Corp. v. Excel Communications*, 52 U.S.P.Q.2d 1865 (D. Del. 1999).

7. 35 U.S.C. §102.

8. 35 U.S.C. §103.

9. 35 U.S.C. §112 ¶1 (1994).

10. Ibid.

11. One classic justification for having a patent system is to encourage inventors to disclose their ideas to the public, who will benefit from this new knowledge once the patent expires. *Kewanee Oil Corp. v. Bicron Corp.*, 416 U.S. 470, 489 (1974) (referring to the "federal interest in disclosure" embodied in the patent laws); see also Edith Tilton Penrose *The Economics of the International Patent System* (Baltimore: Johns Hopkins University Press, 1951), 31–34.

12. Without the disclosure obligation, patentees could conceivably keep the workings of their inventions secret, relying on that secrecy to extend protection even after the patent has expired. Cf. *Pitney-Bowes v. Mestre*, 701 F.2d 1365, 1372 n.12 (11th Cir. 1983) (discussing the policy concerns here).

13. *State Indus. v. A.O. Smith Corp.*, 751 F.2d 1226, 1236 (Fed. Cir. 1985) ("One of the benefits of a patent system is its so-called 'negative incentive' to 'design around' a competitor's products, even when they are patented, thus bringing a steady flow of innovations to the marketplace."); Craig Allen Nard, "Toward a Pragmatic Textualist Approach to Claim Interpretation," *Harvard Journal of Law and Technology* 14 (2000): 1 [§II.C.2] ("The practice of designing around extant patents creates viable substitutes and advances, resulting in competition among patented technologies. The public clearly benefits from such activity").

14. See, e.g., Mark A. Lemley, "The Economics of Improvement in Intellectual Property Law," *Texas Law Review* 75 (1997): 989; Robert P. Merges, "Intellectual Property Rights and Bargaining Breakdown: The Case of Blocking Patents," *Tennessee Law Review* 62 (1994): 75; Robert P. Merges and Richard R. Nelson, "On the Complex

Economics of Patent Scope," *Columbia Law Review* 90 (1990): 839; Suzanne Scotchmer, "Standing on the Shoulders of Giants: Cumulative Research and the Patent Law," *Journal of Economic Perspectives* 5 (1991): 29; Jerry R. Green and Suzanne Scotchmer, "On the Division of Profit in Sequential Innovation," *RAND Journal of Economics* 26 (1995): 20; Suzanne Scotchmer, "Protecting Early Innovators: Should Second-Generation Products be Patentable?" *RAND Journal of Economics* 27 (1996): 322; Howard F. Chang, "Patent Scope, Antitrust Policy, and Cumulative Innovation," *RAND Journal of Economics* 26 (1995): 34; James B. Kobak Jr., "Intellectual Property, Competition Law and Hidden Choices between Original and Sequential Innovation," *Virginia Journal of Law and Technology* 3 (1998): 6; Clarisa Long, "Proprietary Rights and Why Initial Allocations Matter," *Emory Law Journal* 49 (2000): 823.

15. See *Fonar Corp. v. General Electric Co.*, 107 F.3d 1543, 1549 (Fed. Cir. 1997); see also Lawrence D. Graham and Richard O. Zerbe Jr., "Economically Efficient Treatment of Computer Software: Reverse Engineering, Protection, and Disclosure," *Rutgers Computer and Technology Law Journal* 22 (1996): 61, 96–97; Anthony J. Mahajan, "Note, Intellectual Property, Contracts, and Reverse Engineering after ProCD: A Proposed Compromise for Computer Software," *Fordham Law Review* 67 (1999): 3297, 3317.

16. 908 F.2d 931 (Fed. Cir.), cert. denied, 111 S. Ct. 296 (1990).

17. Ibid., 941–42.

18. Ibid.

19. 107 F.3d 1543 (Fed. Cir. 1997).

20. Ibid., 1549 (citations omitted).

21. *Robotic Vision Sys., Inc. v. View Eng'g, Inc.*, 112 F.3d 1163 (Fed. Cir. 1997) (best mode); *In re Dossel*, 115 F.3d 942 (Fed. Cir. 1997) (written description).

22. *Union Pacific Resources v. Chesapeake Energy Co.*, 236 F.3d 684, 690-91 (Fed. Cir. 2001).

23. One recent decision even found that a specification that provided inconsistent guidance as to how the invention worked was not indefinite. See *S3 Corp. v. Nvidia Corp.*, 259 F.3d 1364 (Fed. Cir. 2001); compare ibid., 1371 (Gajarsa, J., dissenting).

24. See 35 U.S.C. §112, ¶6.

25. For an example, see *In re Alappat*, 33 F.3d 1526 (Fed. Cir. 1994) (en banc).

26. Ibid.

27. On the perils of reverse engineering patented software, see Cohen and Lemley, "Patent Scope and Innovation," 17–21. Cited in note 2.

28. Compare *In re Vaeck*, 947 F.2d 488 (Fed. Cir. 1991) (levels of experimentation and skill in the art in obviousness test) with *In re Wands*, 858 F.2d 731 (Fed. Cir. 1988) (levels of experimentation and skill in the art in enablement test). See also Donald S. Chisum, "Anticipation, Enablement and Obviousness: An Eternal Golden Braid," *AIPLA Quarterly Journal* 15 (1987): 57 (discussing the fundamentally interrelated nature of the obviousness and enablement inquiries).

29. 425 U.S. 219 (1976).

30. 107 F.3d 1565 (Fed. Cir. 1997).

31. 239 F.3d 1343 (Fed. Cir. 2001).

32. In *In re Zurko*, 111 F.3d 887 (Fed. Cir. 1997), the CAFC held that a patented software invention was nonobvious even though each of the elements of the invention could be found in the prior art, where the prior art did not identify the problem to be solved. While *Zurko* certainly demonstrates that some software patents will be held nonobvious, it is a specific holding of rather limited utility to most software patentees.

33. 107 F.3d at 1570.

34. *Amazon.com v. Barnesandnoble.com*, 239 F.3d 1343, 1366 (Fed. Cir. 2001).

35. See also *Electronic Planroom v. McGraw-Hill Cos.*, 135 F. Supp. 2d 805 (E. D. Mich. 2001).

36. See, e.g., Robert P. Merges, "As Many as Six Impossible Patents before Breakfast: Property Rights for Business Concepts and Patent System Reform," *Berkeley Technology Law Journal* 14 (1999): 577; Julie E. Cohen, "Reverse Engineering and the Rise of Electronic Vigilantism: Intellectual Property Implications of 'Lock-Out' Technologies," *Southern California Law Review* 68 (1995): 1091, 1179; Glynn S. Lunney Jr., "E-Obviousness," *Michigan Telecommunication and Technology Law Review* 7 (2000–2001): 363.

37. Cohen, ibid. See also Cohen and Lemley, "Patent Scope and Innovation," 42–44, cited in note 2; Greg Aharonian, http://www.bustpatents.com. But cf. John R. Allison and Mark A. Lemley, "Who's Patenting What? An Empirical Exploration of Patent Prosecution," *Vanderbilt Law Review* 53 (2000): 2099, 2131–32 (software patents actually cite slightly more nonpatent prior art than other types of patents).

38. See Chisum, "Anticipation, Enablement and Obviousness." Cited in note 28.

39. See *Wilson Sporting Goods v. David Geoffrey & Assoc.*, 904 F.2d 677 (Fed. Cir. 1990).

40. 256 F.3d 1323 (Fed. Cir. 2001).

41. Ibid.

42. 102 F.3d 1214 (Fed. Cir. 1996).

43. Ibid. at 1222. To similar effect as *Alpex* is *Wiener v. NEC Elec., Inc.*, 102 F.3d 534 (Fed. Cir. 1996). In that case, the CAFC upheld the district court's finding of noninfringement under the doctrine of equivalents, because there were substantial differences between the patent's requirement that a computer program "call on" columns of data one byte at a time and the defendant's product, in which the columns alleged to be equivalent were not in the data matrix, and therefore were not called on to read data. The court rejected the "conclusory" declaration of plaintiff's expert that the two processes were identical.

44. 149 F.3d 1335 (Fed. Cir. 1998).

45. 197 F.3d 1377 (Fed. Cir. 1999).

46. Ibid. at 1386. See also *Netword LLC v. Centraal Corp.*, 58 U.S.P.Q.2d 1076 (Fed. Cir. 2001) (claim requiring caching of data by local servers that pulled information from a central registry not infringed under the doctrine of equivalents by a system in which all local computers hold full copies of the central registry).

In a related context (interpreting equivalent structure in a means-plus-function claim), the court held that Nintendo's video game systems did not infringe GE's television switch patents because the patents, written in means-plus-function format, did not disclose a function for the switches identical to Nintendo's function. *General Electric Co. v. Nintendo Co.*, 179 F.3d 1350 (Fed. Cir. 1999). On how the doctrine of equivalents differs from equivalence under a means-plus-function analysis, see *Chiuminatta Concrete Concepts, Inc. v. Cardinal Indus.*, 145 F.3d 1303 (Fed. Cir. 1998).

47. 194 F.3d 1261 (Fed. Cir. 1999).

48. 184 F.3d 1339 (Fed. Cir. 1999).

49. For an argument that a variety of structural tendencies are likely to drive the courts to read software patent claims broadly under the doctrine of equivalents, see Cohen and Lemley, "Patent Scope and Innovation," 39–50. Cited in note 2.

50. See ibid., 40–42; Peter S. Menell, "Tailoring Legal Protection for Computer Software," *Stanford Law Review* 39 (1987): 1329, 1369–70; Pamela Samuelson et al., "A Manifesto Concerning the Legal Protection of Computer Programs," *Columbia Law Review* 94 (1994): 2308, 2376.

51. For more on the reuse of existing code, both within and across companies, see Mark A. Lemley and David W. O'Brien, "Encouraging Software Reuse," *Stanford Law Review* 49 (1997): 255, 261–66.

52. In 1965, Gordon Moore, cofounder of Intel, observed that, historically, the speed of microprocessors had doubled every year. See Webopedia, "Moore's Law" (March 22, 1998), at http://www.webopedia.come/TERM/M/Moores_Law.html. The current definition of *Moore's Law*, as this phenomenon has been dubbed, is that data density doubles every eighteen months (ibid.). It is well known that data storage capacity and transmission rates have shown similarly exponential increases.

53. See Lemley and O'Brien, "Encouraging Software Reuse," 265. Cited in note 51.

54. For the same reason, reverse engineering has had a respected place as a legitimate means of creating interoperability. Virtually all recent copyright decisions have endorsed reverse engineering in some circumstances. See, e.g., *DSC Communications Corp. v. DGI Techs., Inc.*, 81 F.3d 597, 601 (5th Cir. 1996) (holding that the manufacturer was unlikely to succeed on the merits of its claim that a competitor infringed a copyright on an operating system when it downloaded software onto microprocessor cards for testing); *Bateman v. Mnemonics, Inc.*, 79 F.3d 1532, 1539 n.18 (11th Cir. 1996) (affirming acceptability of reverse engineering code); *Lotus Dev. Corp. v. Borland Int'l, Inc.* 49 F.3d 807, 817–18 (1st Cir. 1995) (Boudin, J., concurring) (endorsing reverse engineering); *Sega Enters. Ltd. v. Accolade, Inc.*, 977 F.2d 1510, 1527–28 (9th Cir. 1992) (holding that disassembly is fair use within the scope of that exception under copyright law); *Atari Games Corp. v. Nintendo of Am., Inc.*, 975 F.2d 832,

843–44 (Fed. Cir. 1992) (refusing to find reverse engineering to be copyright infringement); *Vault Corp. v. Quaid Software Ltd.*, 847 F.2d 255, 270 (5th Cir. 1988) (holding unenforceable a provision in a license agreement prohibiting reverse engineering); *Mitel, Inc. v. Iqtel, Inc.*, 896 F. Supp. 1050, 1056–57 (D. Colo. 1995), aff'd. on other grounds, 124 F.3d 1366 (10th Cir. 1997) (endorsing the Ninth Circuit's approach in *Sega v. Accolade*).

55. See notes 50–57 and the accompanying text (making these points in more detail).

56. For a contrary view, see Patrick K. Bobko, "Open-Source Software and the Demise of Copyright," *Rutgers Computer and Technology Law Journal* 27 (2001): 51, 58–60 (arguing that the ratio of development to imitation costs in software is extremely high). It is trivially easy to counterfeit existing software, but it is illegal under copyright law, and the relevant costs are the costs of legal imitation under a regime without patents.

57. Hewlett and Packard and Jobs and Wozniak are the classic examples, but the story has taken on a life of its own. See, e.g., Micalyn S. Harris, "UCITA: Helping David Face Goliath," *John Marshall Journal of Computer and Information Law* 18 (1999): 365, 375.

58. See, e.g., Cohen and Lemley, "Patent Scope and Innovation." Cited in note 2.

59. See Scotchmer, "Standing on the Shoulders of Giants," 29. Cited in note 14.

60. Copyright law is the predominant protection for software, but trade secret and contract law also provide protection. One factor militating in favor of stronger intellectual property protection in software is the ease of duplication of digital information in the networked world. Copyright protection is much better suited to preventing exact duplication than patent protection, however. Copyright law has also been modified to better prevent such copying in the computer context by allowing copyright owners to control access to copy-protected works. See The Digital Millennium Copyright Act, 17 U.S.C. §1201 (2003).

61. Cohen and Lemley, "Patent Scope and Innovation," 39–50. Cited in note 2.

62. Ibid., 54–56.

63. For a detailed discussion, see Samuelson et al., "A Manifesto," cited in note 50; Pamela Samuelson, "CONTU Revisited: The Case against Copyright Protection for Computer Programs in Machine-Readable Form," *Duke Law Journal* (1984): 663, 733.

64. See generally Richard R. Nelson, "Intellectual Property Protection for Cumulative Systems Technology," *Columbia Law Review* 94 (1994): 2674 (arguing for a moderate protection scheme to meet the protective needs of the software industry).

65. Pamela Samuelson worries that software patents may be too broad, given the incremental nature of software innovation. Samuelson et al., "A Manifesto" 2345–46, cited in note 50; see also Samuelson, "Benson Revisited," cited in note 2 (arguing against protecting software with patents). As noted later, we share this concern but believe that the solution is to narrow the scope of those patents.

Some might object to a large number of software patents because they increase the transaction costs of inventing. We are not persuaded, however, that software patents of modest scope will increase transaction costs much more than software copyrights do. The only relevant patents are those that are licensed or litigated—less than 5 percent of the total number—not the whole universe of patents. See Mark A. Lemley, "Rational Ignorance at the Patent Office," *Northwestern University Law Review*, 95 (2001): 1495, 1507. If those patents are of modest scope, they do not present opportunities for their owners to impede largely unrelated technologies, and the transaction costs should be relatively modest.

66. Robert P. Merges, "Uncertainty and the Standard of Patentability," *High Technology Law Journal* 7 (1992): 1.

67. See ibid., 29–32.

68. See *Pfaff v. Wells Elecs.*, 525 U.S. 55, 67–69 (1998).

69. See *Robotic Vision Sys. v. View Eng'g*, 249 F.3d 1307, 1311–13 (Fed. Cir. 2001).

70. The success of the open source movement suggests that significant innovation can occur in the software industry in the absence of intellectual property protection, although it does not follow that we would get as much or the same kinds of innovation were we to abolish intellectual property protection for software outright. For discussions of the open source movement, see Yochai Benkler, "Coase's Penguin, or, Linux and the Nature of the Firm," *Yale Law Journal* 112 (2002): 369; David McGowan, "Legal Implications of Open-Source Software," *University of Illinois Law Review* (2001): 241.

71. James Bessen and Robert Hunt find that software patents tend to be issued to manufacturing companies, not software developers, and that they are consistent with strategic "patent thicket" behavior. James Bessen and Robert M. Hunt, "An Empirical Look at Software Patents" (working paper 03-17/R, http://www.phil.frb.org/files/wps/2003/wp03-17.pdf May 2003). If they are correct, it is further evidence that the scope of software patents should be reduced to eliminate the overlap problem.

72. Dan L. Burk and Mark A. Lemley, "Is Patent Law Technology-Specific?" *Berkeley Technology Law Journal* 17 (2002): 1155, 1202–5.

73. See, e.g., ibid. (suggesting cost and uncertainty of postinvention development as a new secondary consideration supporting nonobviousness).

74. See, generally, Richard R. Nelson, "Intellectual Property Protection for Cumulative Systems Technology," *Columbia Law Review* 94 (1994): 2674 (discussing the need to reduce the scope of patents in the software industry).

75. See note 54 and the accompanying text.

76. Maureen A. O'Rourke, "Toward a Doctrine of Fair Use in Patent Law," *Columbia Law Review* 100 (2000): 1177.

77. See, e.g., U.S. Patent No. 5,179,765 (issued Jan. 19, 1993) (for a "Plastic Paper Clip").

78. 35 U.S.C. §112 (2000).

79. Samuelson and her colleagues argue that certain features of computer programs are readily apparent to competitors and are therefore vulnerable to copying. Samuelson et al., "A Manifesto," cited in note 50, 2333. Their argument, however, depends not only on the vulnerability of programming innovations to casual inspection but also on the ability of competitors to reverse engineer and analyze the design know-how lying "near the surface" of a program. Ibid., 2335–37. If patent law precludes reverse engineering, it also precludes this sort of knowledge. It is true that certain types of computer program innovations, particularly user interfaces, are necessarily available to even the casual user, at least in part. It is unlikely, however, that these innovations are the most significant parts of a new computer program or the parts most likely to be patented. Further, those innovations for which precise understanding is most important (such as application program interfaces) are also those that will not be available to casual inspection.

80. See notes 16-27 and the accompanying text.

81. 35 U.S.C. §271(a) (2000).

82. We should be clear that we are concerned primarily with reverse engineering by "decompilation," that is, working backward from the object code to construct a simulacrum of the source code. Other forms of reverse engineering, such as "black-box" reverse engineering, do not involve making even temporary copies of the program, although they certainly involve "using" it. Our discussion of "reverse engineering" should be understood to refer to decompilation, not to black-box reverse engineering.

83. For further discussion of the implied license and exhaustion doctrines that confer such a right, see Cohen and Lemley, "Patent Scope and Innovation," 30–35. Cited in note 2.

84. Keith E. Witek, "Software Patent Infringement on the Internet and on Modern Computer Systems—Who Is Liable for Damages?" *Santa Clara Computer and High Technology Law Journal* 14 (1998): 303, 323–24.

85. Cohen and Lemley explain how the doctrines of exhaustion and experimental use might be modified to create a right to reverse engineer patented software. Cohen and Lemley, "Patent Scope and Innovation," 29–35. Cited in note 2

86. See ibid., 23–25.

87. See Burk and Lemley, "Is Patent Law Technology-Specific?" Cited in note 72.

88. Grant Gilmore, *The Ages of American Law* (New Haven: Yale University Press, 1977), 95.

89. See *Brooktree Corp. v. Advanced Micro Devices*, 977 F.2d 1555 (Fed. Cir. 1992).

90. See Mark A. Lemley et al., *Software and Internet Law* (New York: Aspen, 2000), 411 (making this point).

91. Cf. 35 U.S.C. §103(b).

92. See *In re Ochiai*, 71 F.3d 1565 (Fed. Cir. 1995).

93. See Mark D. Janis and Jay P. Kesan, "US Plant Variety Protection: Sound and Fury . . . ?" *Houston Law Review* 39 (2002):727; Stephen M. Maurer, P. Bernt Hugenholz, and Harlan J. Onsrud, "Europe's Database Experiment," *Science* 294 (2001); 789.

94. See Guido Calabresi, *A Common Law for the Age of Statutes* (Cambridge, Mass.: Harvard University Press, 1982).

95. See Suzanna Sherry, "Haste Makes Waste: Congress and the Common Law in Cyberspace," *Vanderbilt Law Review* 55 (2002): 309 (arguing that the common law rulemaking is better suited to rapid technological change).

96. See Daniel A. Farber and Philip P. Frickey, "The Jurisprudence of Public Choice," *Texas Law Review* 65 (1987): 873.

97. On the unnecessary complexity of the copyright laws, see Jessica Litman, *Digital Copyright* (Amherst, Mass.: Prometheus Books, 2001), 25; Jessica Litman, "Revising Copyright Law for the Information Age," *Oregon Law Review* 75 (1996): 19, 22–23; Jessica Litman, "The Exclusive Right to Read," *Cardozo Arts and Entertainment Law Journal* 13 (1994): 29, 34 (1994).

98. In particular, 35 U.S.C. §103(b) (biotechnological processes), §155A (private patent relief), §156 (pharmaceutical patent term extension), and §287 (medical process patents).

99. The Hatch-Waxman provisions, 35 U.S.C. §156, in particular have been used on numerous occasions to violate the antitrust laws. Pharmaceutical patent owners have colluded with putative generic entrants to prevent that company or any other from entering the market. See *Andrx Pharms, Inc. v. Biovail Corp.*, 256 F.3d 799 (D.C. Cir. 2001); *In re Cardizem* CD Antitrust Litigation, 105 F. Supp. 2d 682 (E.D. Mich. 2000).

100. Gilmore, "Ages of American Law," 96. Cited in note 88.

101. Ibid.

102. The antitrust laws are an obvious example of the latter. The few sentences of Sherman Act sections 1 and 2, 15 U.S.C. §§1–2 (2000), have spawned a vast set of judicially created standards for identifying and punishing anticompetitive behavior.

103. See, e.g., Richard Gilbert and Carl Shapiro, "Optimal Patent Length and Breadth," *RAND Journal of Economics* 21 (1990): 106 (emphasizing the importance of patent scope to incentives); Robert P. Merges and Richard R. Nelson, "On the Complex Economics of Patent Scope," *Columbia Law Review* 90 (1990): 839 (same).

104. See Calabresi, *A Common Law*, 46–47. Cited in note 94.

105. Ibid., 48.

106. See *Dickinson v. Zurko*, 527 U.S. 150, 161–62 (1999).

107. See Rochelle Cooper Dreyfuss, "The Federal Circuit: A Case Study in Specialized Courts," *New York University Law Review* 64 (1989): 1.

5

State Street Meets the Human Genome Project: Intellectual Property and Bioinformatics

Iain M. Cockburn

Bioinformatics, the burgeoning scientific discipline of computational biology, poses some interesting and difficult questions for intellectual property (IP) policy. By applying computer science and mathematics to databases built around DNA and protein sequence information, this new discipline has made important contributions to modern biology; and it seems likely to play a critical role in the future development of bio-medical science. The intellectual and economic payoff from this cross-fertilization and boundary-spanning activity is likely to be very significant. But as universities and commercial entities seek to acquire intellectual property rights over bioinformatics tools and techniques, this new area has the potential to reignite some old, painful, and unresolved controversies in the patent arena: Situated at the intersection of two of IP policy's most controversial and difficult areas—algorithmic inventions and molecular biology—bioinformatics may be particularly sensitive to developments in legal doctrine and Patent Office practice.

This chapter reviews potential causes for concern arising from these debates and presents some preliminary statistics on patenting in bioinformatics. Interestingly, relatively few patents have been granted in this area, and there is little evidence (so far) of the types of "bad" outcomes seen in other technologies, such as the explosion of apparently trivial business method patents seen in the late 1990s, the issuance of overly broad patents like the infamous Compton multimedia case,[1] or the development of extensive patent thickets that inhibit technology development.[2] Arguably, this reflects the constraints on patenting imposed by a vigorous "open source" community engaged in developing software tools for bioinformatics, whose activity serves to protect the public domain.[3]

What is *bioinformatics*? The term was first coined in the 1980s to refer to analysis of sequence data, although molecular biologists had begun making discoveries by building databases of biological information and developing algorithms to analyze them decades earlier. While classic bioinformatics focused on the analysis of sequence information to identify genes and their functions, "new" bioinformatics extends the use of computational methods as tools of scientific discovery into even more ambitious contexts. Computational methods are now being used to predict and characterize protein structures and interactions and even more broadly to manage and interpret collections of linked clinical and molecular data.[4]

This in silico research, conducted in computers rather than in test tubes, plays a vital role in realizing benefits from the raw data generated by genome sequencing. Without bioinformatics tools, the vast amounts of new data now being generated on DNA sequences, molecular structures, disease correlations, and population variation are useless. For example, insight into the genetic basis of disease depends on the ability to identify meaningful patterns in DNA sequence data, which has been enabled by the development of search and comparison algorithms such as BLAST.[5] Web-enabled searches of sequence information using BLAST are reported to exceed 60,000 per day; and though claims that modern biology is now "essentially a BLAST application" are exaggerated, they illustrate the degree to which this technology has become an essential tool for biomedical research.[6] Bioinformatics therefore continues to receive substantial support from public research funding agencies: the National Library of Medicine (which encompasses the National Center for Biotechnology Information) alone requested more than $325 million for the fiscal 2005 federal budget. The area has also attracted significant private sector investment: Worldwide several hundred venture-backed enterprises are dedicated to commercial development or exploitation of bioinformatics, and the area is a major focus for many other pharmaceutical and biotechnology companies.

Patenting Activity in Bioinformatics

Given the fluid nature of the field, a precise measure of patenting activity in bioinformatics is very difficult to obtain. An approximate gauge is given by the number of patents classified as both "software" and "molecular biology," although the exercise of counting patents in either of these areas is far from straightforward.[7] Building on prior research, I obtained the set of software patents applied for in the United States between 1990 and 2003 using the search algorithm for "software" developed by Graham and Mowery augmented to include business methods and obtained the equivalent set of patents for "molecular biology" using a search algorithm based on that developed by Walters et al. to count DNA patents, augmented by terms designed to capture new scientific usage and the domains of proteomics and protein structure data.[8]

Figure 5-1 plots the annual count of patents granted in the United States that fall in the intersection of these two sets of patents. Interestingly, the number of patents classified as both software and molecular biology is very small. Using these fairly generous definitions, approximately 48,000 "molecular biology" patents and approximately 220,000 "software" patents were issued in the United States between 1990 and 2003 but only 305 fall in both sets. Of these, about half claim the results of using computational techniques to identify specific genes or therapeutic compounds. Only 148 of these 305 patents appear to be "pure" bioinformatics inventions in the sense of claiming general purpose algorithms or methods. Note though the significant increase after 1997: These statistics point to a significant surge in patenting activity in the bioinformatics area. The dropoff in counts after 2000 reflects the delay between filing an application and eventual issuance of a patent during which the application is examined by the Patent Office. Once applications filed in recent years move through the Patent Office and appear as granted patents, counts for 2000 onward can be expected to rise substantially compared to those reported here. Figure 5-2 shows the results of performing the same search used for figure 5-1 but of published U.S. applications rather than issued patents. The results indicate that significant numbers of bioinformatics patents are in the pipeline, although many of these applications may take many years to issue or may not survive examination.

It is important to recognize that the counts of patents presented here are surely an underestimate of the total amount of patenting activity relevant to

FIGURE 5-1

ISSUED U.S. BIOINFORMATICS PATENTS (by filing date)

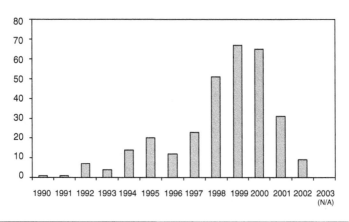

SOURCE: United States Patent and Trademark Office; author's calculations.

bioinformatics. An unknown but potentially large number of patents classified only as software or only as molecular biology may be highly relevant to bioinformatics. For example, U.S. Patent 6,108,666, "Method and Apparatus for Pattern Discovery in 1-Dimensional Event Streams," appears to be very closely related to methods used to identifying biologically relevant patterns in nucleotide or amino acid sequences (and cites many papers in biology journals as prior art) but is classified only in data-processing categories.[9]

Gene Patent Issues Revisited?

The central role played by genomic information in generating potentially commercially valuable discoveries has meant that questions of access to and control over sequence databases, and the nature of patent rights in genes, have been highly controversial.[10] In the 1990s, fears were widely expressed that patents would be issued on large amounts of DNA sequence data, conferring potentially very broad rights to exclude other researchers from working not just on the genes encoded by these sequences, but also the proteins

FIGURE 5-2

PUBLISHED U.S. BIOINFORMATICS PATENT APPLICATIONS (by filing date)

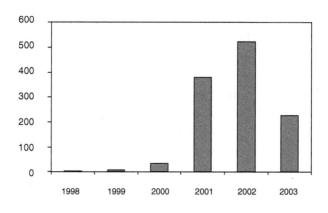

SOURCE: United States Patent and Trademark Office; author's calculations.

expressed by them and "downstream" diagnostic and therapeutic applications. Heated debate erupted over the patentability of isolated gene fragments or single base-pair mutations without well-defined functions as tens of thousands of patent applications on "ESTs" and "SNPs" were filed by companies such as Incyte, Celera Genomics, and Human Genome Sciences.[11]

These concerns have subsided, somewhat, in the wake of strengthened examination criteria requiring applicants to demonstrate "specific, substantial, and credible" utility and legal decisions that have narrowed the scope of patent claims on genetic sequences by establishing fairly stringent standards for disclosure and enablement in biotechnology patents.[12] But a number of fundamental controversies about gene patents are essentially unresolved. For some commentators, gene sequencing is a process of discovery rather than invention and should not therefore be rewarded with patents. For others, many gene patents do not meet standards of nonobviousness.[13] For example, objections have been raised to granting patents on genetic sequences that code for a known protein, on the grounds that sequence of amino acids in the protein necessarily implies a nucleotide sequence (or rather a set of possible nucleotide sequences). And, notwithstanding the federal appellate court's history of treating genetic discoveries as purely chemical inventions, the fundamental duality of DNA molecules as both repositories of data and compositions of matter has left the courts and the Patent Office in the uneasy position of, effectively, allowing patents on information.[14]

Bioinformatics is intimately connected to these issues. Algorithms for comparing sequence homologies can play a vital role in establishing utility, provided the Patent Office accepts some degree of similarity with sequences of known function as establishing credible functionality of the claimed sequence. But, since gene sequences can now be found with minimal human intervention through software-supported automated sequencing of DNA and the use of algorithms that automatically "mine" the resulting data for regions that actively code for proteins, it is highly debatable whether or not any "invention" in the sense of creativity or originality is taking place. Considerable effort and creativity may have gone into devising the hardware that performs the automated sequencing and the software that identifies genes, but arguably, none has gone into the "discovery" of gene sequences identified by this system.

Implications of *State Street*

As software, bioinformatics tools have been patentable subject matter in the United States for many years, although interest in obtaining patents on algorithms and processes appears to have sharply increased since 1998, following the *State Street* decision in the Court of Appeals of the Federal Circuit (CAFC).[15] This decision was interpreted as affording patent protection to more general algorithms or mathematical principles, provided they generate useful and tangible results. Returning to figure 5-1, it is tempting to attribute the sharp increase in applications for bioinformatics patents after 1997 solely to the *State Street* decision, but this was also a time of accelerating technological activity in the field, driven by the intensification of efforts to sequence the human genome, explosive growth of the Internet and computing power, and other factors. Therefore, it is far from clear how much, if any, of the increase is due to *State Street*.[16]

Nonetheless, as algorithmic inventions, bioinformatics patents are likely to be controversial in much the same way that software and business methods patents have been. These include difficulties in searching prior art, poor quality control and uneven standards of review at the Patent Office, and rejection by the relevant community of practice of the standards applied by the Patent Office and the courts to evaluate nonobviousness and novelty. Though issued in large numbers in the United States for many years now, software patents continue to generate acrimonious debate.[17]

Challenges Posed by a Frontier Technology

Bioinformatics illustrates some general difficulties in establishing appropriate IP rules for new, rapidly evolving technologies. Any new technology presents the patent system with transitional difficulties in determining standards of patentability, establishing procedural requirements, and developing legal doctrine to address idiosyncratic aspects. These may be satisfactorily resolved with the passage of time and sufficient accumulation of experience, but while courts and administrative entities wrestle with these difficult questions, large numbers of applications can build up in the Patent Office and eventually start issuing. Under the statutory presumption of validity, these patents can strongly affect the nature of ongoing research, the direction of development of the technology, and the cast of players. In this case, the situation is further complicated by the new area inheriting unresolved patent issues from its parent disciplines, compounded by the boundary-spanning nature of bioinformatics.

As a scientific discipline, bioinformatics combines knowledge from traditional "wet biology," statistics, mathematics, computer science, database management, and other areas. Examination of bioinformatics patent applications therefore requires examiners to search and integrate knowledge of prior art in very different domains of expertise. Hopefully patents will not be issued in large numbers for claims to existing software techniques applied in the bioinformatics context. Unfortunately, the experience to date with business methods does not instill optimism: Notwithstanding strong statements by the Patent Office to the effect that claims to "well known business methods but implemented over the internet" would not be allowed, only limited creativity in drafting claims seems to have been required to get patents of this type issued.[18]

As an example of the difficulties that could arise at the confluence of biology and business methods, consider the following hypothetical claim:

A business method comprising: (a) identifying the locations of disease related single nucleotide polymorphisms in the human genome by comparing the frequency of patterns of such variation in the DNA of a control group of individuals in a disease group with their frequency in the DNA of individuals in a healthy control group, (b) using said identified locations in a discovery process, and (c) marketing products from said discovery process.

This example is greatly simplified: As written, the novelty of claim elements (a) and (b), in and of themselves, is highly questionable, but if this claim were allowed, any use of a process that contains all three elements would constitute infringement.[19] Thus, the patent holder would be able to exclude others from marketing *any* drug discovered using the scientific method laid out in elements (a) and (b). As written, this claim amounts to a patent on the idea of being a genomics-based drug company. Even if the combination of elements (a) and (b) constituted a novel scientific method, from an economic perspective, the inventiveness in the addition of element (c) appears to be de minimis. Yet allowing such a claim would confer a very large span of economic control on the patent holder. Further, it is trivially easy to come up with variations on claim element (c) that are business processes relating to the commercialization of drugs discovered using (a) and (b), such as "entering into a strategic alliance with a manufacturing and marketing partner," "raising investment funds to pursue clinical development," or "taking orders for products discovered using said process via an electronic network." This is an exaggerated and artificial example, and as written, it would appear to be unlikely to survive the patent application process.[20] But it illustrates the potentially serious consequences of attributing sufficient novelty, utility, and nonobviousness to combinations of scientific processes with business processes to allow them to be patented.

As biological research, the practice of medicine, and the business of pharmaceuticals are becoming increasingly abstract and overlapping activities, the Patent Office therefore faces some serious challenges in developing and applying appropriate standards for determining the novelty of boundary-spanning claims. Furthermore, because bioinformatics melds biology and software, applicants have plenty of room to exploit differences across the two technologies in standards for obviousness, disclosure, and enablement. In biotechnology, jurisprudence and Patent Office practice have resulted in relatively stringent requirements for enablement and disclosure and a relatively low hurdle for nonobviousness.[21] In software and business methods, the enablement and disclosure requirements set by the Patent Office appear to have been relatively lax, resulting in issuance of patents with broader claims.[22]

We should therefore expect patentees to strategically emphasize the biology aspects of the patent over the algorithmic aspects, or vice versa, raising the likelihood of the Patent Office's making a mistake in examination and making the economic "reach" of bioinformatics patents very difficult to assess.[23] Examples such as the software patent on "Pattern Discovery in 1-Dimensional Event Streams" discussed earlier (which has no references to biology but appears to be highly relevant to bioinformatics) suggests that the dual nature of bioinformatics inventions can make these patents unusually difficult to find in the course of routine searches.

These difficulties in identifying and evaluating patents in this new domain may result in significant costs. On the one hand, to the extent that the dual nature of bioinformatics gives applicants an unusual advantage in "gaming" the examination process, they may be able to obtain socially suboptimal quantities of patents of questionable validity.[24] On the other hand, uncertainty about the scope of claims, such as that surrounding the applicability of an "information technology" patent to a problem in biology (or vice versa), may leave both the patent holder and potential infringers uncertain about its enforceability. This is likely to raise the amount and the cost of litigation. All else equal, hidden patents tend to raise costs associated with defending against opportunistic "surprise attacks"; firms operating in the area may have to expend considerable resources to definitively determine their freedom to operate through exhaustive searches in unfamiliar technological domains.

Assessing the Impact

The consequences of growing numbers of bioinformatics patents for the pace of innovation in the field, for levels of investment in new ventures, and for other economically significant metrics are hard to predict. Much depends on the evolution of legal doctrine and standards, but with the exception of DNA chips and arrays (which are a hardware aspect of bioinformatics), litigation in this area has yet to become a high-profile issue.

Indeed, litigation activity in bioinformatics has been quite limited to date. Of the 148 patents identified earlier, only 2 are reported by Lexis/Nexis to be the subject of litigation. One of these was among the handful of objectionable patents in bioinformatics identified in the National Academies' recent patent reform proposals[25]; however, the judge dismissed the case with prejudice. The other was asserted in conjunction with several other hardware/chemical patents in a dispute about DNA arrays that was subsequently settled with no legal findings as to validity and enforceability. At less than 1 percent, this rate of litigation is much lower than the 6 percent reported by Lerner for the patents assigned to a sample of 530 biotechnology firms during the early 1990s, but it is difficult to interpret this figure given the limited time that has passed since these patents were issued.[26]

Judicial interpretation of boundary-spanning claims in bioinformatics patents is therefore difficult to predict. Indeed, much of the uncertainty surrounding the strength of patent protection for algorithms and business processes in the wake of *State Street* is yet to be resolved. Relatively few business method patent infringement suits have been decided, and where cases have been brought, the scope of algorithmic claims tends not to be tested. Some bioinformatics patents do appear to be very broad. For example, consider U.S. Patent 6,633,819 "Gene Discovery Through Comparisons of Networks of Structural and Functional Relationships Among Known Genes and Proteins" issued to Columbia University. The abstract of this patent describes the invention as relating to "methods for identifying novel genes comprising: (i) generating one or more specialized databases containing information on gene/protein structure, function and/or regulatory interactions; and (ii) searching the specialized databases for homology or for a particular motif and thereby identifying a putative novel gene of interest . . . the invention may further comprise performing simulation and hypothesis testing to identify or confirm that the putative gene is a novel gene of interest." On the face of it, this patent appears to cover a large fraction of all activity in bioinformatics and genetic research! However, closer examination of the actual claims of patents such as these reveals them to be much narrower in scope than their titles or abstracts suggest.

A review of the trade press in this area suggests that in silico analogs to the very broadly applicable and widely licensed patents on foundational "wetware" technologies such as Columbia's "Axel" patents on cotransformation or Stanford/UCSF's "Cohen-Boyer" patents on gene-splicing have yet to emerge. This absence of outrage suggests that, if broad blocking patents have been issued in bioinformatics, they are either not being asserted or are being licensed on uncontroversial terms.[27]

It should also be noted that, while bioinformatics inherits some of the "bad" aspects of patenting in its parent technologies, it also inherits some of the "good." Software and business methods patents have frequently been criticized for failing to cite relevant nonpatent prior art. Even though published prior art may just be particularly difficult to find in these areas, Patent Office practice may also be a source of such "errors." Operating under tight resource constraints and performance quotas, patent examiners often appear to confine their searches for prior art to sources that are familiar and easy to search.[28] In practice, this can mean issued and pending patents. While applicants have a legal duty to supply all prior art of which they are aware, they also have limited incentives to do so. By contrast, molecular biology patents typically list voluminous quantities of references to academic papers and other publications. In part, this strikingly different practice reflects the area's close links to academic science or, indeed, applicants' employment in academic institutions but may also indicate the presence of exhaustively indexed and easily searchable repositories of nonpatent literature such as the PubMed database. Most of the 148 patents identified here as "bioinformatics" appear to follow the norms of molecular biology, citing the academic literature copiously. In this sense, at least, bioinformatics may not be vulnerable to the "quality" problems experienced in software and business methods.

Economic Context

Bioinformatics is a "tool" technology, used to discover products that are subsequently sold to end users, rather than a "product" in and of itself. The economic returns realized on investment in bioinformatics will therefore to a great extent be driven by the terms under which downstream entities focused on developing salable products are able to access or practice the technology. Intellectual property rights and the strength and scope of patents will clearly play an important role in determining these terms of access. But they will also reflect the interplay of business models and industry structure in the bioinformatics producing and using sectors, and the economic significance of bioinformatics can be understood only in relation to these aspects of the commercial environment.

Commercial activity in bioinformatics followed a variety of paths. Companies focused purely on the information technology (IT) aspects of bioinformatics tended to follow one of three models. Software developers such as Silicon Genetics developed bioinformatics packages for visualization, annotation, and analysis of sequence data, which are sold and distributed in ways very similar to other types of software. A second model, exemplified by application service provider (ASP) companies such as Doubletwist and Compugen, is that of hosting and selling access to comprehensive integrated bioinformatics platforms.[29] A third model for specialist companies, followed by companies like LION bioscience, is to provide expertise and proprietary data architectures to assist third parties in integrating and streamlining access to disparate databases and technology platforms. Interestingly, IT specialists like IBM, HP, Hitachi, and Motorola, which have not previously been directly associated with innovation in biotechnology, play an increasingly important role in this area.

Companies that combine innovation in bioinformatics with research directed toward end-product development fall into two groups: those such as Incyte and Curagen that have sold access to their proprietary data and tools in parallel to their internal drug discovery efforts, and those that develop data and tools for internal use. While patents based on sequence information have played an important role in the past for some of these companies, much of the value associated with their investments in bioinformatics appears to be protected by trade secrets, rapid product development, and the ability to maintain exceptionally high-quality data.

All commercial activity in bioinformatics is powerfully constrained, however, by a vibrant and vigorous effort in the public domain, much of which follows the "open source" model.

Open Source Biology

Efforts to capture value from bioinformatics through proprietary rights over source data or algorithms have been limited by the active development and publication of databases and software created by researchers and institutions that emphasize collaborative effort, unrestricted access, and prompt publication of data and code.[30] Once in the public domain, source code, documentation, and (annotated) sequence data are a source of prior art that can be used to reject or limit subsequent patent applications.

As far as databases are concerned, bioinformatics relies heavily on taxpayer-funded, openly accessible public repositories of sequence data such as the GenBank/DDBJ/EMBL database supported by the International Nucleotide Sequence Database Collaboration. These databases depend critically on community norms and the policies of granting agencies and academic journals, which have enforced prompt and regular deposits of data.[31] Without guarantees of government funding, however, these initiatives appear to be difficult to sustain, and they are subject to the usual difficulties in motivating and coordinating collective action.[32] For example, since the Swiss government dropped its support, the long-established Swiss-Prot database has struggled to find a commercial business model that satisfies demands for open access by the public sector researchers who largely created the data while covering costs of maintenance and distribution. Furthermore, just as the most widely known open source software projects (Linux and the GNU applications) are, to a large degree, the creatures of Linus Torvalds and Richard Stallman, development of some critical bioinformatics databases has relied heavily on the vision, values, and commitment of single individuals or small groups. For example, the value of the Swiss-Prot database is acknowledged to be derived to a great extent from having been actively "curated" or "edited" by its founder, Amos Bairoch.[33] Obviously these models are fragile and have bounded processing capacity.

Interestingly, not all of the "open" databases rely exclusively on public funding sources. Industry funding has supported a number of open database initiatives, dedicated to developing and maintaining collections of data in the public domain with unrestricted access. The most notable of these is the SNP Consortium in which the Wellcome Trust and eleven pharmaceutical companies collectively obtained and put into the public domain large quantities of data on single nucleotide polymorphisms, the smallest unit of genetic variation among members of the same species. Some genomics companies have also been willing, at least in principle, to cover costs of maintaining and distributing databases in return for limited periods of exclusive use of new contributions to the database or rights to be the exclusive access point.[34] But mixed motives underlie industry funding: "Downstream" firms have clear incentives to limit "upstream" property rights,[35] and since information in open databases is likely to be complementary to that held in closed proprietary databases, these expenditures on expanding open access data may have the effect of raising the economic value of privately held data. Again, without guarantees of continued financial support, the long-term viability of such arrangements is questionable.

On the analysis and algorithmic side of bioinformatics, researchers in both public sector and private sector organizations have been active collaborators in creating a variety of freely available software applications with published source code. These include projects that create and maintain applications such as BLAST or Ensembl for searching and annotating sequence data; projects that develop suites of software tools, subroutine libraries, and programming languages such as BioPerl, BioJava, BioPython, and BioSQL; and efforts to develop protocols and standards such as DAS (distributed annotation system) or OBDA (open biological database access) that promote integration and interoperability of disparate technology platforms. Provided the Patent Office is willing to track and search the source code and documentation of these projects, they would appear to be a powerful limitation on the ability of independent developers to obtain extensive patent rights over bioinformatics software.[36]

There are important differences, however, between "open" and "open source" development of databases and software. The open source development model emphasizes integration of collective effort from independent contributors as well as unrestricted access and depends critically on the ability to enforce restrictions on modification and reuse that assure open access to the results of ongoing development. "Open" projects, such as BLAST software and the Genbank/DDBJ/EMBL database, have released source code and data into the public domain with no restrictions on use or modification. Therefore, nothing prevents for-profit entities from incorporating this public domain code and data in closed, proprietary products.

In contrast, open source projects are typically distributed under the "copyleft" model, using the GNU public license (GPL) or variants on it.[37] Some important examples of bioinformatics applications or application suites licensed under the GPL or similar provisions are EMBOSS, Ensembl, BioPerl, Rasmol, and a large number of smaller or more specialized open source bioinformatics applications. Under most forms of these licenses, while the project is not put in the public domain, access to it is unrestricted, in that any entity can use, copy, redistribute, resell, or modify the source code—but only on condition that the provisions of the license are retained. Modifications or additions to the source code are therefore automatically made available to the public. This "viral" property effectively prevents the output of open source projects from being incorporated into closed proprietary products: Commercial developers would find it difficult to recoup the costs of making any additions or improvements if they were obliged to provide unrestricted access to them. The Human Genome Organization reportedly considered, but did not implement, the open source model for sequence data. Had it done so, Celera Genomics would have faced an interesting dilemma: In its effort to produce a proprietary sequence database of the human genome, the company made extensive use of publicly funded sequence data in open databases.[38]

The enforceability of the GPL and other "copyleft" licenses is currently unclear. The pending *IBM v. SCO* case, where "copyleft" and GPL licensing are receiving their first substantial legal test, would therefore appear to have significant implications for the bioinformatics sector.

Another important aspect of "openness" lies in the arena of standards and standard setting. Open, extensible, software standards play a particularly important role in bioinformatics, where the value of any single piece of sequence or structure information is greatly enhanced by the ability to cross-reference across multiple databases. Arguably, proprietary data structures or encoding standards protected by patents would seriously impede innovation or impose substantial costs of duplication and work-arounds. Antitrust authorities have scrutinized the potential drawbacks of patent holders' controlling industry standards quite carefully in a number of cases involving IT.[39] No such cases have yet emerged in bioinformatics, but the experience of organizations such as the World Wide Web Consortium (W3C) and the Internet Engineering Task Force suggest that the bioinformatics community does not face an easy task.[40] Institutions will need to be developed to identify potential attempts to "hijack" software standards through patents, and the community will also need to wrestle with difficult questions relating to governance and participation in bodies set up to define and regulate such standards.

Conclusion

Bioinformatics now plays a central role in both fundamental biological research and commercial efforts to translate the massive volumes of biological data now available into useful drugs and diagnostics. On the face of it, by combining two of the most controversial and difficult areas of patent law and practice (gene patents and software/business methods), the bioinformatics field would appear to be unusually susceptible to bad outcomes from the patent system. But the specter of "hijacking the genome" through proprietary rights to source data or inappropriately broad blocking patents on fundamental algorithms for interpreting genetic sequence data appears, at least so far, to have been avoided.

Limiting patent rights is not, of course, costless. While academic science is flourishing in this area, commercial organizations are presumably relying increasingly on secrecy, copyright, and other mechanisms to protect their investments in bioinformatics tools and data. To the extent that increased reliance on secrecy limits access by the entire research community and that progress in the area depends on linkages among data sources and interoperability of software tools, there is obviously cause for concern. Nonetheless, the pace of technological development remains high in bioinformatics, and obvious problems arising from holding critical data secret are difficult to identify, at least at present.

This state of affairs is contingent on a number of factors. First, the Patent Office must meet the challenge of maintaining high levels of quality in examination of patents that span rapidly evolving fields with very different histories of development, inconsistent standards of patentability, and disparate sources of prior art. Second, judicial standards for determining the scope of claims to algorithmic inventions are yet to be fully developed. As with any new technology, these must carefully balance the incentives of early versus follow-on inventors.[41] Third, the continuing contribution of public domain/open access bioinformatics databases and software tools as an important check on overextension of exclusionary rights into this fundamental technology must be assured. Efforts to create and maintain these important resources currently have considerable momentum, although the vitality of the "open biology" community that creates and supports them depends critically on the maintenance of social norms, the availability of sufficient resources to maintain and distribute databases and source code, open standards for data exchange, and the robustness of legal devices such as the GPL that support open source development.

Notes

1. Compton's Newmedia and Encyclopedia Britannica were issued U.S. Patent 5,241,671 "Multimedia Search Systems Using a Plurality of Entry Path Means Which Indicate Interrelatedness of Information" in 1993, generating a storm of protest and an unusual commissioner-ordered reexamination. See John Markoff, "Patent Office to Review a Controversial Award," *New York Times*, December 17, 1993, D2. Notwithstanding subsequent Patent Office statements that the patent had been canceled, it was eventually reissued in July 2002 with much more limited claims.

2. On thickets, see Carl Shapiro, "Navigating the Patent Thicket: Cross Licenses, Patent Pools and Standard Setting," in *Innovation Policy and the Economy*, vol. 1, ed. Adam Jaffe, Joshua Lerner, and Scott Stern (Cambridge, Mass.: MIT Press/NBER, 2001). Robert Merges and Richard Nelson, "On the Complex Economics of Patent Scope," *Columbia Law Review* 90 (1990): 839–916, and Seth Shulman, *Unlocking the Sky: Glenn Hammond Curtiss and the Race to Invent the Airplane* (New York: HarperCollins, 2002) provide historical cases of broad patents blocking innovation.

3. *Open source* refers to a mode of innovation that emphasizes unrestricted access, widespread publication and distribution of source code, peer-reviewed collaborative development, and reciprocal sharing of improvements, enforced by community norms and legal devices such as "copyleft" licensing agreements, which permit reuse and modification, provided the results are subsequently made available to the public under the same terms as they were obtained.

4. Andreas Baxevanis and B. F. Francis Ouellette, *Bioinformatics: A Practical Guide to the Analysis of Genes and Proteins*, 2d ed. (New York: Wiley, 2001), and C. W. Sensen, ed., *Essentials of Genomics and Bioinformatics* (New York: Wiley, 2002) are useful introductory texts on bioinformatics.

5. BLAST, the Basic Local Alignment Search Tool, is a widely used algorithm and software implementation for searching for matches or homologies in sequence information, developed at the National Center for Biotechnology Information. Other important algorithms are ssearch and FASTA.

6. It is interesting to speculate on where modern biology would be today if broad patents covering the BLAST algorithm had been obtained by a for-profit company that, as with Myriad Genetics and the BRCA1 breast cancer gene, was unwilling to license them. "Bad" outcomes from a sufficiently broad blocking patent would include limiting the number of individuals and institutions that participated in developing methods for compiling and searching genome data, thus slowing technological progress; a fragmented and inefficient infrastructure built on incompatible work-arounds; or even a relocation of bioinformatics activity to jurisdictions that do not recognize the patent. On the other hand, such an attempt to monopolize a critical resource might have resulted in redoubled effort to develop alternate methods and quick development of superior noninfringing technology.

7. Patent titles and abstracts can be surprisingly misleading, and the technology classes assigned by patent offices to help in searching are far from transparent and do not map readily into economic notions of technologies. Skilled searchers can readily identify patents that are "close" to a specific piece of technology, but there is surprisingly little consistency in the size of broad technology classes defined by academic researchers for various purposes. For example, keyword searches such as used by James Bessen and Robert Hunt, "An Empirical Look at Software Patents" (working paper no. 03-17/R, Federal Reserve Bank of Philadelphia, 2003), for software may overestimate patents in a particular class, while classification code searches may underestimate the total.

8. See Stuart Graham and David Mowery, chapter 3 in this volume; Stuart Graham and David Mowery, "Intellectual Property Protection in the U.S. Software Industry," in *Patents in the Knowledge-Based Economy*, ed. Wesley Cohen and Stephen Merrill (Washington, D.C.: National Academies Press, 2003); Leroy Walters et al., *The DNA Patent Database* (2004), available at http://dnapatents.georgetown.edu/.

9. In principle, patents such as these could be found by expanding the search strategy described previously to include nonpatent references to prior art. But other potentially highly relevant patents are much harder to find. Careful tracing of citation patterns can uncover patents containing claims that appear to cover bioinformatics software techniques but do not cite the biology literature, such as U.S. patent number 5,819,266 "System and Method for Mining Sequential Patterns in a Large Database," but this is very difficult to do other than on a case-by-case basis.

10. See among many others, "HUGO Warning over Broad Patents on Gene Sequences," *Nature* 387, no. 6631 (1997): 326; John Barton, "Intellectual Property Rights: Reforming the Patent System," *Science* 287 (2000): 1933–34; John Barton, "Rational Limits on Genomic Patents," *Nature Biotechnology* 18 (2000): 805; Nuffield Council on Bioethics, *The Ethics of Patenting DNA* (London: Nuffield Council on Bioethics, 2002).

11. ESTs, expressed sequence tags, merely point to the presence of genes at a particular point in a DNA sequence, rather than giving the full sequence of the gene or any indication of its function. SNPs, single nucleotide polymorphisms, are the minimal unit of genetic variation among members of the same species. Differences in a single base pair among the many thousands constituting a whole gene have been identified as responsible for diseases such as cystic fibrosis. See Bruce Alberts, "Letter from the President of the National Academy of Sciences to the U.S. Secretary of Commerce Concerning EST Patents," reprinted in *Plant Molecular Biology Reporter* 15, no. 3 (1997): 205–8; Rebecca Eisenberg, "Do EST Patents Matter?" *Trends in Genetics* 14, no. 10 (1998): 379–81.

12. Among the key cases are *Enzo v. Calgene*, 188 F.3d 1362 (Fed. Cir. 1999), and *The Regents of the University of California v. Eli Lilly*, 119 F.3d 1559 (Fed. Cir. 1999).

13. Appeals court decisions (*In re Bell* and *In re Deuel*) have effectively lowered the standard of obviousness to a minimal level when applied to genetic sequences, in sharp contrast to European practice.

14. See Rebecca Eisenberg, "Re-Examining the Role of Patents in Appropriating the Value of DNA Sequences," *Emory Law Journal* 49 (2000): 783–800.

15. Prior to this case (*State Street Bank & Trust Co. v. Signature Financial Group Inc.*, 149 F.3d 1368, CAFC, 47 USPQ2d 1596 [Fed. Cir. 1998]), most practitioners and legal texts held to the view that business methods were not patentable. In its decision, the court emphatically laid to rest what it described as the "ill-conceived" business methods exception. This was shortly followed by another important ruling in *AT&T Corp. v. Excel Communications, Inc.*, 172 F.3d 1352, 50 USPQ2d 1447 (Fed. Cir. 1999), confirming that no associated physical transformation activity was necessary for patentability of algorithms.

16. Indeed, only a handful of the sample of 48,000 "molecular biology" patents referred to previously are also explicitly classified as a "business method."

17. See David Burton, "Software Developers Want Changes in Patent, Copyright Law" (1994), available at http://lpf.ai.mit.edu/Whatsnew/survey.html; USPTO, *Hearings on Software Patent Protection* (Washington, D.C.: U.S. Patent and Trademark Office, January–February 1994); Kenneth Dam, "Some Economic Considerations in the Intellectual Property Protection of Software," *Journal of Legal Studies* 24 (1995): 321–77; Robert Hunt, "You Can Patent That? Are Patents on Computer Programs and Business Methods Good for the New Economy?" *Federal Reserve Bank of Philadelphia Business Review* Q1 (2001): 5–15; and Pamela Samuelson, Randall Davis, Mitchell D. Kapor, and J. H. Reichman, "A Manifesto Concerning the Legal Protection of Computer Programs," *Columbia Law Review* 94 (1994): 2307–2431.

18. See Michael Meurer, "Business Method Patents and Patent Floods," *Washington University Journal of Law and Policy* 8 (2002): 309–43, and Bronwyn Hall, "Business Method Patents, Innovation, and Policy" (mimeo, Department of Economics, University of California–Berkeley, 2003).

19. Subject to any limitations in the scope of the claim implied by the extent of enablement in the patent and its prosecution history.

20. The claim language of this example paraphrases some of the pending U.S. applications from a company that, paradoxically, is highly innovative, attracting substantial venture capital funding to work at the frontier of computational biology using state-of-the-art information technology to manipulate and analyze terabytes of data obtained from high-throughput whole genome sequencing of large numbers of clinical trial participants.

21. To obtain a patent, the applicant must disclose sufficient information about the invention to allow others to practice it, without "undue" experimentation. Among other things, this "enablement" requirement prevents applicants from claiming things they hope to invent rather than things they have actually invented.

22. See Dan Burk and Mark Lemley, "Is Patent Law Technology-Specific?" *Berkeley Technology Law Journal* 17 (2002): 1155–1206; Robert Merges, "As Many As Six Impossible Patents before Breakfast: Property Rights for Business Concepts and Patent System Reform," *Berkeley Technology Law Journal* 14 (1999): 577–615; Dan Burk, "Patent Disclosure Doctrines: Enablement and Written Description," Public Hearings on Competition and Intellectual Property Law and Policy in the Knowledge-Based Economy (Washington, D.C.: Federal Trade Commission, 2002).

23. See Josh Lerner, "The New New Financial Thing: The Sources of Innovation Before and After *State Street*" (NBER working paper no. 10223, NBER, Cambridge, Mass., 2004) for discussion of strategic applicant behavior in a different context.

24. As Mark Lemley, "Rational Ignorance at the Patent Office," *Northwestern University Law Review* 95 (2001): 1495, points out, costs associated with issuing poor-quality patents need to be balanced against the resource burden of operating an error-free examination process.

25. Stephen Merrill, Richard Levin, and Mark Myers, *A Patent System for the 21st Century* (Washington, D.C.: National Academies Press, 2004), 36.

26. Josh Lerner, "The Importance of Trade Secrecy: Evidence from Civil Litigation" (working paper no. 95-043, Harvard Business School, 1995); Jean Lanjouw and Mark Schankerman, "Enforcement of Patent Rights in the United States," in *Patents in the Knowledge-Based Economy,* ed. Wesley Cohen and Stephen Merrill (Washington, D.C.: National Academies Press, 2003), report an overall rate of filing suit of about 2 percent for all patents.

27. Another interpretation would be that the community of practice in this area is inured to controversial patents, which no longer attract the volume of comment observed in past decades.

28. See Iain M. Cockburn, Sam Kortum, and Scott Stern, "Are All Patent Examiners Equal? The Impact of Examiner Characteristics on Patent Statistics and Litigation Outcomes" (NBER working paper no. 8980, NBER, Cambridge, Mass., 2002), on the patent examination process.

29. The ASP model is commonplace in commercial data processing. For a fee, the ASP provides storage and computation power to remotely host its clients' data and applications.

30. See, for example, the "Bermuda principles" adopted by participants in the international Human Genome Organization, which required that sequence data and annotations be placed in the public domain, have unrestricted access, and be uploaded to repositories within 24 hours: www.gene.ucl.ac.uk/hugo/bermuda.htm.

31. See, Rebecca Eisenberg, "Genomics in the Public Domain: Strategy and Policy," *Nature Reviews: Genetics* 1, no. 1 (2000): 70–74; Dan Burk, "Open Source Genomics," *Boston University Journal of Science and Technology Law* 8 (2002): 254.

32. See Stephen Maurer, "Inside the Anti-Commons: Academic Scientists' Struggle to Commercialize Human Mutations Data, 1999–2001," *Research Policy*, available at http://socrates.berkeley.edu/~scotch/commercializedata.pdf.

33. Bairoch has been supported in this activity by experts at the Swiss Institute for Bioinformatics and the European Bioinformatics Institute. Other frequently cited examples of critical biological information resources created as "one-man shows" are the REBASE Restriction Enzyme Database created by Nobel Laureate Richard Roberts, and Victor McKusick's OMIM (Online Mendelian Inheritance in Man) database on human genetic diseases.

34. In 2000, Incyte Pharmaceuticals was reported to be willing to contribute several million dollars to support the Human Genome Organization's Mutations Database Initiative. Maurer, "Inside the Anti-Commons." Cited in note 32.

35. See Ajay Agrawal and Lorenzo Garlappi, "Public Sector Science and the 'Strategy of the Commons,'" *Best Paper Proceedings of the Academy of Management* (Briarcliff Manor, N.Y.: Academy of Management, 2002), CD-ROM.

36. Discussion of advances in bioinformatics in the large, accessible, and exhaustively indexed biomedical literature should also serve as a source of prior art that will effectively limit patent rights.

37. The Open Source Initiative has approved more than forty open source license agreements. See www.opensource.org.

38. See John Sulston and Georgina Ferry, *The Common Thread: A Story of Science, Politics, Ethics and the Human Genome* (Washington, D.C.: National Academies Press, 2002).

39. See Carl Shapiro and Michael Katz, "Antitrust in Software Markets," in *Competition, Innovation and the Microsoft Monopoly: Antitrust in the Digital Marketplace*, ed. Jeffrey Eisenach and Thomas Lenard (Boston: Kluwer Academic Press, 1999), for discussion of relevant antitrust issues.

40. Anxiety over the potential consequences of patents on key WWW protocols such as P3P (Platform for Privacy Prefences) or XrML (digital rights management extensions) led the W3C to develop a formal policy for licensing of consortium members' patents covering technology embodied in WWW standards. After intense and controversial debate in the relevant technical communities about proposed "reasonable and non-discriminatory" licensing, the organization adopted a policy that makes "essential claims" of relevant patents issued to participants in working groups developing standards automatically available to the public on a royalty-free basis. The policy also contains provisions requiring timely disclosure of patent applications, rules for exceptions, and penalties for failing to comply.

41. See Suzanne Scotchmer, "Standing on the Shoulders of Giants: Cumulative Research and the Patent Law," *Journal of Economic Perspectives* 5, no. 1 (1991): 29–41; Ted O'Donoghue, Suzanne Scotchmer, and Jacques Thisse, "Patent Breadth, Patent Life, and the Pace of Technological Improvement," *Journal of Economics and Management Strategy* 7 (1998): 1–32.

6

"Open and Collaborative" Research:
A New Model for Biomedicine

Arti K. Rai

The advent of open source software has prompted theoretical speculation about the applicability of open source innovation principles to biomedical research. This chapter moves beyond theoretical analysis into an empirical examination of existing projects that operate under an "open and collaborative" model. Open and collaborative projects often diverge from traditional open source innovation, particularly in terms of restrictions on participation, need for public funding, and use of "copyleft" licensing. Nonetheless, they represent a fresh approach to biomedical research in that they reject its exclusionary behavior and small-lab-based structure. Open and collaborative biomedical research is a potentially valuable experiment. It has produced software and genomic data that can freely be used by follow-on innovators. The model may also allow a more coordinated and comprehensive attack than has heretofore been possible on the sorts of problems that cause promising drug candidates, particularly for complex diseases, to fail. On the other hand, if the open, collaborative experiment is going to succeed, particularly in the wet lab arena, proponents must recognize the need to retain downstream patents and either work within or attempt to change publishing norms in biological science.

Copyright 2005 by Arti K. Rai. I thank Jamie Boyle, Iain Cockburn, Wesley Cohen, Bob Hahn, and participants at the April 30, 2004, AEI-Brookings workshop on Intellectual Property Rights in Frontier Industries: Software and Biotech for very helpful comments. A longer version of this paper is available at http://papers.ssrn.com/sol3/papers.cfm?abstract_id=574863.

In the last twenty-five years, biomedical research has become increasingly proprietary[1] and secretive.[2] Given the cumulative nature of research, this trend has raised fears that future progress may be impeded by access and licensing difficulties. One important response has involved calls for improving access by requiring scientists and research institutions to put data and certain types of research tools into the public domain or, at a minimum, license them widely and nonexclusively at a reasonable fee.[3] This emphasis takes the current organizational structure of research as a given but seeks to reduce the intensity of exclusionary behavior associated with the research. A more dramatic response has begun to emerge, however. Public funding bodies, prominent scientists, and even some pharmaceutical firms have taken steps in the direction of what might be called *open and collaborative*[4] science. Open and collaborative projects both disavow exclusionary behavior and move beyond the traditional small-lab-based structure of biomedical research.

The rise of arguments for open and collaborative biomedical research has coincided with two phenomena: (1) the increased importance of computation in such research;[5] and (2) the well-documented emergence of so-called open source methods of innovation in computation-heavy areas of research and development, primarily software. In some recent cases, the modeling on open source software has been quite explicit; for example, the federally funded haplotype mapping project, which aims to create a database that catalogues human genetic variation, has adopted a licensing policy that is self-consciously modeled on the "copyleft" system of open source software licensing.[6] Under the copyleft version of open source development, users can access source code freely, but such access is conditioned on the user's making his improvements to such information available under the same conditions.

Although some commentators have theorized about the application of "open source" principles to biomedical research,[7] they have not analyzed carefully how this model is actually being used. In this chapter, I use information gathered through empirical investigation of existing projects to offer observations on how the open and collaborative model actually works. The projects encompassed by this label vary quite substantially. Some closely resemble open source software while others diverge rather significantly, particularly in four respects: restrictions on participation, degree of centralization and standardization, reliance on public funding, and use of "copyleft" licensing.

Whether the open and collaborative model is likely to promote socially desirable biomedical innovation,[8] either as an absolute matter or relative to more traditional exclusionary models, is a difficult question to answer. Because the model is quite fresh, and the time delay before research on this model can be translated into end products is long, empirical demonstration of the model's virtues and vices, at this stage, probably is impossible.

Nonetheless, there are reasons to believe that the model is worth pursuing. Not only has it produced software and genomic data that are usable, but the resulting public domain status for this software and data can reduce transaction costs and secrecy that may impede the follow-on research that leads to end products. The model's least intuitive but most exciting application may involve "wet lab" systems biology: In this context, the model may allow a more-coordinated and -comprehensive attack on large, complex problems than traditional small-lab biology. Given that the dearth of knowledge regarding systems biology appears to be an important reason many promising drug candidates, particularly for complex diseases, currently fail in preclinical or clinical trials,[9] open and collaborative approaches may be welcome news even to those industries that favor strong intellectual property protection, such as the pharmaceutical industry.[10]

Certain applications of the open and collaborative model, however, raise concerns. One concern involves the possibility of reduced incentives for development and commercialization as research moves downstream, toward the chemical compound that will be the drug candidate. As various empirical studies have documented, patents on chemical compounds are critical for recouping the large costs associated with preclinical and clinical R & D.[11] To preserve development and commercialization opportunities, there is reason to be cautious about copyleft licensing, at least outside the context of software. The first section of this chapter gives economic and institutional background on biopharmaceutical innovation, with an eye toward highlighting transaction cost and secrecy concerns to which the open and collaborative model aims to respond. The next section discusses how large-scale collaboration has operated in the context of software and some other Web-based information projects. It also discusses preliminary results from empirical investigation of some prominent open and collaborative biomedical research

projects. Then, I use these results as well as the theoretical literature to eluci-
date the extent to which the open and collaborative model may produce
socially desirable biomedical innovation. In this section, I also make recommendations for removing institutional obstacles in those cases where the
model may be superior to alternative arrangements.

The Open and Collaborative Model in Context

Innovation in Biopharmaceuticals. For much of the twentieth century,
biopharmaceutical innovation largely comprised trial and error by large,
vertically integrated pharmaceutical firms. Through a combination of size
and monopoly-conferring end product patents, these firms hedged the risk
associated with their trial-and-error-based innovation. Biomedical research
science operated in a different world, linked more closely to the realm of
philosophy than the realm of commerce. This is not to say that biomedical
science necessarily adhered in all respects to the norms of scientific com-
munalism described by sociologists like Robert Merton.[12] The authors of
one recent study that reanalyzes data from the 1960s argue that, even in
1966, experimental biologists were more reluctant than scientists in other
fields to discuss ideas freely outside their individual lab.[13] Nonetheless, the
secrecy that existed was fueled by academic competition, not commercial
competition.[14]

In the middle to late 1970s, the advent of recombinant DNA and mono-
clonal antibody research caused the conceptual gap between research science
and the therapeutic products of interest to industry to shrink. Just as university research was becoming interesting to industry, Congress passed the Bayh-
Dole Act of 1980, which aimed to encourage downstream commercialization
by allowing patenting and exclusive licensing of federally funded discoveries.[15] The Court of Appeals for the Federal Circuit, created in 1982, further
encouraged proprietary trends in basic biomedical research by relaxing the
so-called utility and nonobviousness requirements for patentability.[16] Finally,
over the last ten years, with the infusion of genomic and proteomic information, biopharmaceutical innovation has become perhaps even more science
intensive. All pharmaceutical firms aim to produce drugs by systematically
testing their drug compound libraries on genomic and proteomic "targets."

The consequences of these changes have been dramatic. Universities can, and often do, patent upstream research.[17] So do small firms and startups. In the case of universities, licensing upstream research produces revenue. For small firms and startups, upstream patents, or exclusive licenses to upstream university patents, appear to be important for attracting venture capital and securing revenues when licensed to large pharmaceutical firms. Even for research that is not patented, upstream players may leverage their physical control over the data or tool to exact reach-through royalties. For their part, large pharmaceutical firms, once vertically integrated engines of innovation, must now negotiate a complex array of university and small firm proprietary claims on research inputs. While some of these claims may be narrow in scope,[18] other claims may be broader.[19] Significantly, with the increasing importance of computation, particularly software, in biomedical research, software is now another category of patented research tool that may add to upstream complexity.

Vertical "Dis-Integration" and Calls for Access. As noted, property rights on upstream research inputs have fostered the creation of small firms that market such inputs. To the extent that small firms may be more innovative than large firms,[20] and thus produce research inputs better and faster than large firms, this change could be positive. Additionally, to the extent that research inputs are licensed widely to interested downstream developers, the creation of a market for such inputs could conceivably increase downstream competition. On the other hand, as economist Ronald Coase would predict,[21] the move away from the vertically integrated firm has increased transaction costs substantially. Although such increases do not appear to have caused ongoing projects to stop,[22] there is some evidence that firms, including small firms that aim to move downstream, may avoid research areas where there are significant patent positions.[23] Additionally, in at least some cases, patent rights on research inputs have been licensed exclusively. Although exclusivity might be appropriate when a particular input needs further investment for development and commercialization, some of these cases have involved situations where the exclusive right has been asserted to block the marketing of end products that downstream developers were able to make without the need for exclusivity.[24]

Moreover, problems associated with even purely academic access appear to have become more prevalent.[25] With respect to data and materials to which researchers need physical access, both increased commercialization and increased scientific competition among labs have contributed to access difficulties. According to a 1997 study, 20 percent of academic respondents delayed publication for more than six months, either for reasons related to commercialization (for example, the need for secrecy before a patent application is filed or the desire for trade secrecy)[26] or because of scientific competition.[27] A 2002 study found that even access denials related to published research were prevalent; in 21 percent of cases, such denials caused the academic investigator to abandon a promising line of research.[28] Once again, both commercial considerations and academic competition were cited as reasons for access denials.[29] For materials that academic researchers can readily reproduce on their own, some of these researchers have been able to secure an informal regime of price discrimination by simply ignoring patent rights. Whether this informal price discrimination regime will survive the Federal Circuit's decision in *Madey v. Duke* to eliminate any possibility of an infringement exemption for research is unclear.

Beyond Access: Open and Collaborative Research

As the web of upstream proprietary rights and secrecy has grown, various public and private sector groups have made calls for greater access to research tools. Given the problems that may be created by new proprietary rights and are almost certainly created by ever-increasing levels of secrecy, calls for access are important. Indeed, in the biological sciences, such calls for access may even create a Mertonian sphere more robust than that which existed before 1980. One step beyond such calls, however, is the open and collaborative model. This model is Mertonian in the sense that scientists work openly, without secrecy and the usual sorts of exclusionary proprietary rights. But it goes beyond Merton in that it explicitly requires scientists to work closely with others outside their own lab or small firm. Requiring scientists to work closely with others, in larger groups than is ordinarily the case, responds to a set of problems that involve not only intellectual property rights but also science policy. Specifically, because complex diseases involve multiple interactions between multiple genes and proteins, understanding these diseases may require the coordinated work of more than a small lab or firm.

In this section, I describe a variety of existing open and collaborative biomedical research projects. Because many proponents of this research invoke the example of open source software, I first discuss briefly the open source model.

The Open Source Model. Open source software development has its origins in the norm-based Mertonian framework for conducting scientific research. More specifically, the open source movement originated in a communal "hacker" culture that prevailed in certain academic laboratories in the 1960s and 1970s. At that time, packaged software was rare and individuals freely exchanged software and underlying source code for purposes of modification and improvement. Such exchange was facilitated with the creation of the ARPANET network, which eventually expanded into the Internet. Indeed, the transaction cost-lowering properties of the Internet probably allowed Mertonian norms to operate more effectively and in larger groups than they ordinarily operate.[30]

Open source software production differs from Mertonian norms in several respects. One obvious difference is that open source software development operates under the legal framework of a copyright license: The copyright in the source code is the foundation for the license. The open source license, as defined by the Open Source Initiative (OSI), now encompasses over thirty types of copyright licenses for source code. Although the exact terms of these licenses vary and some involve fees for use, they share the requirement that the licensee receive source code and be able to redistribute the source code.[31] As a first approximation, open source licenses can be divided into two categories: "copyleft" or GPL licenses that require licensees who make improvements to the software to make those improvements publicly available on the same open source terms that they received the software,[32] and those that disclose source code but essentially impose few if any requirements on recipients. An argument often made in favor of copyleft licenses is that, by preventing private appropriation of volunteer labor, such licenses provide an incentive for volunteers to contribute in the first instance.[33] The existence of myriad licenses notwithstanding, no case involving an open source license appears to have been litigated to judgment.[34] Rather, according to one study, the primary vehicle for enforcement is identification and critiquing of violations on online mailing lists and bulletin boards.[35] Therefore, this difference from Mertonian norms may be more apparent than real.

A difference that is perhaps more significant lies in mechanisms for information integration. While the Mertonian model does not posit a specific mechanism for information integration, open source software production, particularly production in large-scale projects, often has a central developer or group of developers responsible for evaluating and integrating developments on an ongoing basis. New and modified code deemed to be of sufficient quality by the developer may then be added to the official version of the code.[36] To some extent, the control exercised by the developer resembles that exercised by firm management. On the other hand, entry and exit from developer status are more fluid than entry and exit from firm management. Thus, particularly for large-scale projects, open source software production could be seen as lying somewhere between Mertonian norms and the firm.[37]

Perhaps the most prominent respect in which open source software production differs from Mertonian science is that it is generally *not* funded publicly.[38] To the contrary, certain firms have been built on providing services for open source software. Moreover, according to one recent study of 287 open source projects, 38 percent of open source software developers make their contributions at work, with the knowledge of their supervisors. Presumably, the firms for which these developers work value the specific improvements that the developers make. Perhaps because open source contributors are highly varied in their background, they have a wide variety of intrinsic and extrinsic motivations for contributing: personal enjoyment, sense of community obligation, pay, solving a specific problem, honing skills, and enhancing career prospects.[39] Nonetheless, many open source developers, like the idealized Mertonian scientist, appear to be significantly motivated by the personal enjoyment derived from undertaking creative tasks. To the extent that this hedonic incentive or other nonmonetary incentives substitute for salary, the result can be software production that is significantly cheaper than commercial production.

Proponents of open source software argue that such software development works in the sense that it produces usable output at a lower cost than conventional proprietary development. Some make the more ambitious claim that this output, which large numbers of independent programmers continually examine for defects and the possibility of adding additional features, is likely to be technically superior to closed source output. A small number of technical studies have tested the latter claim. One academic study that compared Linux, Apache, and GCC with their closed-source counterparts appears to buttress claims that open source software may be technically superior. The study determined that open source software had a higher rate of function modification (i.e., fixing of defects) and added more functions over time.[40] Similarly, Reasoning, Inc., a software inspection service, determined in a 2003 report that the Linux TCP/IP stack had fewer defects than commercially developed TCP/IP stacks. Reasoning, Inc.'s analysis found, however, that Apache had as many defects as its commercial counterpart. According to the authors of the latter study, this result may be a consequence of the Apache product's still being relatively early (as compared with Linux) in the software life cycle. Given the heterogeneity of both open and closed source software, attempts to generalize from a small number of case studies are perilous. Nonetheless, these studies show that open source software is a reasonable alternative to closed source, particularly if the end user wants a low price.[41]

In recent years, various large, Web-based collaborative projects have begun to generate outputs other than software. Several technical projects merit discussion because they use mechanisms for integration of information that are less hierarchical than those used in open source software development. One of these, the NASA Clickworkers project, relies on public volunteers to mark craters on Mars. Once contributions of these workers were aggregated by focusing on areas of consensus, their contributions averaged out as comparable to that of trained geologists. The technology magazine *Slashdot* uses a complicated peer rating mechanism to determine the extent to which a contributor's posts will be seen by other users. One recent review of these collaborative projects argues that such projects are likely to be superior to firms and markets in allocating human creativity when the cost to volunteers of contribution is low and such contributions can be readily filtered and aggregated.[42]

The rise of open source software and, more generally, information production through volunteer labor aggregated over the Internet has coincided with the ascendance of computation in biological research. This coincidence has inspired speculation about the possibility that similar approaches could apply to biomedical research. It has also inspired a fair number of open and collaborative projects, particularly in the area of bioinformatics. The remainder of the paper describes these projects and evaluates the extent to which they are likely to (1) produce usable output, (2) alleviate transaction cost and secrecy problems without causing problems for commercialization, and (3) address scientific challenges, particularly challenges surrounding systems biology, that cause drug candidates for complex diseases to fail in preclinical and clinical trials.

Open and Collaborative Biomedical Research. In this section, I describe various efforts at open and collaborative biomedical research. Because the relevant technical, organizational, and economic considerations are distinct, I treat software, databases, and "wet lab" biology as separate categories. The following section then turns to an evaluation of the projects.

Bioinformatics software. Many bioinformatics software projects, particularly small software projects, operate under an open source model. By those who participate in such projects, the open source model is seen as a good mechanism for information dissemination, reduction of duplicative effort, and rapid development of software.[43] By the same token, devotees of open source do not necessarily believe that all bioinformatics software should be open source.[44]

An important difference between most open source software and open source bioinformatics software is that the latter is publicly funded. Moreover, because most research universities require that employee rights in software developed using university resources be assigned to the university,[45] the policy of universities toward open source software development becomes quite relevant.

Preliminary results from interviews with technology transfer offices (TTOs) at twenty universities that have large software patent, biomedical patent, or biomedical research portfolios indicate that most university TTOs have not, at least thus far, been seeking many software patents.[46] The reason is economic: Because software licensing typically yields little in the way of licensing revenues, software does not generally merit the cost of a patent filing. To the extent that universities distribute software, it is through nonexclusive copyright licensing.[47]

Even though they do not typically seek patents, many universities are only beginning to formulate policies with respect to open source software.[48] Two universities that have relatively well-developed policies, the University of Washington and Georgia State, treat software differently depending on whether it is perceived as commercially valuable.[49] For software that is not commercially valuable, the researcher's preference governs. If software is commercially valuable, both universities recommend that software and source code be licensed free of charge to noncommercial users but licensed for a fee to commercial users. Of course, this differentiation between commercial and noncommercial can be maintained only through limits on redistribution of source code. Such limits are in tension with open source principles that counsel against such limits.

A few universities report "bright-line" policies regarding open source software that appear more encouraging to open source. For example, both MIT and Stanford allow different types of open source software licensing if the researcher wants to use that approach.[50] MIT also manages open source licenses for researchers. Similarly, the University of Texas defers in significant part to the licensing preferences of the researcher and also manages the researcher's licenses.[51]

Genomics database projects. The first, and probably still most important, open and collaborative genomic database project was the publicly funded project to sequence the human genome. Unlike traditional human genetics, which revolved around individual laboratories that tended to be highly competitive—and hence uneven in their willingness to share information, particularly prepublication—the Human Genome Project (HGP) was, from the outset, a collaborative endeavor. The intensity of the collaboration increased in 1998, after the project was faced with a challenge from Craig Venter, the leader of a private effort to sequence the genome. To meet this challenge, the public project streamlined the number of participants and further integrated its operations. The major sequencing centers (the so-called G-5) were required to report their progress in weekly conference calls with the funding entities, principally the National Human Genome Research Institute (NHGRI).[52]

True to the nature of the open and collaborative model, the producers of the human genome sequence did not simply put the raw data into public domain. Rather, as the data were produced, an open source software program, known as the distributed annotation system (DAS), was set up to facilitate collaborative improvement and annotation of the genome. DAS has also been applied to other genomes, including mouse, C. elegans, fruit fly, and rice. Under the DAS system, any interested party can set up an annotation server. DAS enables end users of the information—in other words, researchers—to choose the annotations they want to view by typing in the URLs of the appropriate servers. Annotation quality is judged via mechanisms somewhat similar to those employed in the NASA Clickworkers project. Specifically, according to Lincoln Stein, one of the designers of the DAS, it was "designed to facilitate comparisons of annotations among several groups. The idea is that an annotation that is similar among multiple groups will be more reliable than an annotation that is noted by one group."[53] The quality of the annotation is also judged by looking at published papers that describe the annotation technique.

The data dissemination and improvement policy of the HGP and large-scale genome mapping projects more generally was developed by scientists and National Institutes of Health (NIH) administrators and essentially imposed on the administrators of the participating universities. Although universities played no role in formulating the policy, they appear to have acquiesced in the rejection of proprietary rights.[54] Therefore, the NIH did not need to invoke the cumbersome legal procedure set up by Bayh-Dole to restrain university patenting.

Within the HGP, there was some discussion about using some type of "copyleft" license on the data produced by the project.[55] The view among these participants was that such a license would prevent private entities, particularly Craig Venter, from gaining an advantage over the public project by making proprietary any improvements Celera made to the public data. Although the HGP leaders rejected a copyleft approach,[56] NHGRI, together with other funding organizations, quite explicitly adopted a copyleft-style policy in setting up the International Haplotype Mapping Project (HapMap). This project aims to catalog haplotypes (patterns of genetic variation) and link such patterns to disease phenotypes. To identify a particular haplotype, researchers must first identify the individual genotypic variations that make up the haplotype. The HapMap project releases individual genotype data as soon as it is identified. Before haplotype information has been assembled, it may be possible for those who access the data to take these data, combine them with their own genotype data, and generate enough information to file patent applications on haplotypes of interest. To address this possibility, the project set up a "click-wrap" license that requires those who access the HapMap database to agree that they will not file product patent applications in cases where they have relied in part on HapMap data.[57] Although this license does not (and cannot) rely on an assertion of copyright in the underlying data, it does represent an enforceable contract.[58]

Systems biology and "wet-lab" projects. Outside the context of digital information (that is, for projects that require significant wet-lab biology[59]) the open and collaborative model does not appear to have been used widely. However, it may be making some inroads in the context of some recent "systems biology" projects funded by the NIH. In the last five years, the National Institute of General Medical Science (NIGMS) has funded five large grants intended to "make resources available for independently funded scientists to form research teams to solve a complex biological problem that is of central importance to biomedical science . . . and that would be beyond the means of any one research group." These grants depart from the traditional biological grant model, which focuses on individual laboratories.

The Alliance for Cell Signaling (AFCS) was the first of these large grants to be funded. It was inspired by the HGP,[60] and it clearly invokes significant elements of an open and collaborative approach. The alliance is led by Nobel laureate Alfred Gilman of the University of Texas, Southwestern Medical School. Gilman won the Nobel Prize for his work on the role of G proteins in cell signaling, and the goal of the project is to map complex signaling networks. While cell biologists once believed that signals, such as a drug candidate binding to a cell receptor, initiated only one pathway, it is now clear that a chemical stimulus can excite different networks that interact in complex ways. Combinations of ligands can increase complexity even further. The ultimate goal of the experimental work within the AFCS is threefold: first, to catalogue the "parts" (that is, the stimuli and signaling proteins); second, to identify the interactions between these parts; and third, to generate a computational model of signaling within the cell.[61]

The AFCS comprises eight "wet labs" and one bioinformatics lab. Each wet lab measures a distinct aspect of the effect produced by different ligands. The bioinformatics laboratory is responsible for integrating the data produced by the eight wet labs. The leaders of the AFCS have determined that, to generate reliable output that can be meaningfully compared and aggregated across labs, laboratory inputs (e.g., cell lines) and procedures must be standardized. Much work has gone into such standardization, and the protocols used are publicly available on the Web.[62] In addition, the direction of future experiments is agreed on collaboratively, based on the data generated thus far.[63]

Another novel aspect of the AFCS involves its lack of emphasis, at least thus far, on conventional publication through peer-reviewed, printed scientific journals. Rather, after some internal review, data publication takes place expeditiously on the Web.[64] Moreover, although the AFCS investigators replicate experiments and analyze data further, and publish those reviews on the Web as "research reports"[65]—they have no formal "head start" in terms of this analysis. In this respect, the AFCS is explicitly modeled on the HGP. The lack of emphasis on conventional publication also coheres with the organizational structure of the AFCS. While most lab directors are senior tenured professors who have advanced through the conventional career track for academic scientists, many of the individuals who work in the AFCS laboratories are on a different, and in some respects novel, career track: They are postdoctoral scientists who are not planning on tenure-track appointments. Many of these individuals plan to go into private sector research.

On the other hand, the AFCS is beginning to shift toward a more-conventional, print-publication-oriented approach. Some of the lab heads observe that it may be difficult to get scientists outside the AFCS to pay attention to the data generated by the alliance without using the conventional publication route.[66] Indeed, the AFCS website now emphasizes that scientists who use AFCS data can publish their work in peer-reviewed publications; a few in fact have published such work.[67] Nonetheless, among the AFCS lab directors, there is lingering concern that prestigious print publication venues—*Science, Nature, Cell*, and the like—may be reluctant to publish papers associated with data available on the Web prior to publication.[68]

Finally, and perhaps most unusually, all participants in the AFCS agreed to disavow intellectual property rights in their research. This agreement to disavow conventional property rights, quite obviously, is contrary to the trends in patenting we have witnessed since passage of the Bayh-Dole Act. Moreover, many of the institutions participating in the AFCS, perhaps most notably the University of California system but also the University of Texas and the California Institute of Technology, have substantial numbers of patents. It appears that Gilman's Nobel Prize, as well as his stature in the area of cell signaling, enabled him to convince recalcitrant university administrators, particularly at the University of California and the California Institute of Technology, not to interfere in the disavowal of property rights. But even someone of Gilman's stature found the task difficult.[69]

Open and Collaborative Biomedical Research: A Critical Evaluation

This section assesses the extent to which the open and collaborative approach has the potential to produce socially desirable innovation, particularly as compared with more traditional, proprietary approaches.

Open Source Bioinformatics Software. To some extent, the variables involved in the normative evaluation of open source bioinformatics software are similar to those involved in the normative evaluation of open source software generally. Although no technical evaluation of which I am aware has specifically compared open source bioinformatics software with comparable closed source software, the technical superiority of certain types of open source software suggests that, at least in some circumstances, the open source model might yield technically superior bioinformatics software. At a minimum, open source software may be a good alternative for producing an output of reasonable quality at low cost. In addition, academic computational biologists appear to be motivated to contribute to open source software by some of the same incentives that motivate other open source developers: creative pleasure, the desire to solve a specific problem, sense of community obligation, or perhaps even the possibility of consulting revenues. Equally important, the use of open source software, even copyleft software, should not interfere with ordinary scientific kudos incentives. The open source regime allows publication in conventional print journals of articles that either discuss the software or, more likely, discuss biological insights that are gained by using the software (for example, to query a database).

University-based open source production of bioinformatics software is also unlikely to undermine commercial development of such software, whether on an open or closed source model. Unlike small biopharmaceutical firms, small software firms do not appear to rely on exclusive licenses to university patents.[70] As a consequence, even if we assume that small firms are important for generating or disseminating research inputs widely, there is little reason to believe that open source production of software within the university will undermine the formation of small firms.

The main obstacle to experimentation with open source bioinformatics software appears to be institutional. As currently constituted, the financial interests of open source developers and university TTOs may be at odds. To the extent that open source developers derive money from consulting revenues, they may be reluctant to embrace any university restrictions on the availability of source code to potential customers. Indeed, in the last few years, there have been a few celebrated cases where open source bioinformatics software developers have clashed with universities over questions of ownership and licensing. These have been cases in which the researcher derived substantial consulting revenue from open source distribution of the bioinformatics software.[71]

The question of who should be responsible for determining whether a particular piece of bioinformatics software is open source is a difficult one. Nonetheless, an argument can be made in favor of the approach taken by MIT, Stanford, and the University of Texas: deference to researcher choice. Although open source is not necessarily the best approach for all software projects (for example, any blanket NIH mandate to require open source software in its grants would be unfortunate), bioinformatics software developers are probably well placed to determine whether, in any given case, open source development is the best approach as a scientific matter. Moreover, in the context of software, researcher choices are unlikely to impose significant development-impeding externalities (as they arguably did in the pre-Bayh-Dole era): The software itself can be developed through volunteer labor, and it is difficult to imagine how any form of open source licensing, even copyleft licensing, would undermine important patent rights on biochemical compounds, such as genes, proteins, or small molecule chemical drugs. Deference to researchers might be particularly desirable to the extent that researcher preferences were not unduly biased in favor of open source because of the prospect of consulting revenues. For example, universities might ask for the same percentage of consulting revenues that they currently get from licensing revenues. This option would, of course, have the corresponding advantage of not biasing universities against open source.[72]

Open and Collaborative Databases. In several respects, an open and collaborative approach to database generation and improvement has value. Not only does the approach allow for comprehensive database annotation, but it also provides an "infrastructure" of freely available scientific information that all researchers, including wet-lab researchers, can use. Unlike software projects, however, database generation can require substantial capital investment. Although sequencing machines and other tools for generating data have decreased in price, it is unrealistic to imagine that tools for generating data can readily be made available to all interested volunteers. Indeed, in the context of the HGP, efficient production of data required streamlining to a core set of five institutions. In sum, although data generation can be open and collaborative, some restrictions on participation, as well as public funding, will generally be necessary.

In contrast with initial data generation, data annotation can hew more closely to the open source model. In many cases, annotators use publicly available computer algorithms to search existing databases for comparable sequences of known function. Thus, just as with software, the major expense associated with annotation is labor. Indeed, the DAS system used by the public genome projects is in many respects less hierarchical than open source software development.

Because of the high cost associated with generating initial data, and the corresponding value associated with such data, public funding of databases probably undermines the ability of private businesses to form around databases. Unlike software, it is unlikely that private database businesses can be built on a services model. The race to sequence the human genome provided something of a natural experiment for testing the services model. Once the public data were available, the primary value added that Celera could provide was service related. Although a significant number of firms and academic institutions subscribed to the Celera database for these services,[73] the availability of the public data placed a ceiling on what Celera could charge. This ceiling was sufficiently low that Celera has largely moved out of the database business and into drug development. Arguably, the challenge from Celera provided the competition necessary for the public project to streamline its approach. To the extent that Celera's database business failed, we may see fewer challenges of this sort in the future.

Although a strong argument can be made that upstream data should be publicly available, even if such availability requires public funding and undermines private database companies, the case for having such data undermine the availability of patent rights on more downstream improvements generated by data users is weaker. Unlike software patents, patents on drug candidates, and perhaps even downstream research that leads directly to a drug candidate, are unequivocally important in the biopharmaceutical industry. Moreover, while copyleft licensing might be useful for inducing participation in purely volunteer open source projects,[74] it should not be as critical for inducing such participation in projects where the collaborators are publicly funded academics. A statement by prestigious print publications pledging not to discriminate against articles that analyze publicly available data would provide additional incentive: Although data generators and annotators might not have any official head start in submitting those articles, their familiarity with the data should put them in a good position for submitting original analyses. For example, in the case of the Human Genome Project, participants in the project submitted original analyses that were published by *Nature*. Additionally, at least in the long term, it might be appropriate for the biological community to give data generators and annotators publication-type credit for their work, even if the work is placed immediately on the Web and reviewed by peers subsequent to such Web publication rather than prior to it.[75]

Wet-Lab Biology. Thus far, the open and collaborative model's application to wet-lab biology has largely been limited to systems biology. Even this limited application is significant, however. As a scientific matter, there is reason to believe that systems biology will be crucial for certain types of drug innovation, particularly in the context of complex diseases. Moreover, given the limited capabilities of any single lab, collaboration between labs may be necessary for understanding systems biology.

As with initial data generation, the capital costs associated with wet-lab biology are sufficiently high that it probably is inefficient for most wet-lab collaborations to be open to all comers. Indeed, even with a limited number of players, public funding is necessary. Finally, some level of standardization of wet-lab inputs may be important to generate reliable data, especially if such data are going to be aggregated across laboratories. At a minimum, transparency of the protocols used to generate the data is necessary.

Although it may be inefficient for collaborative work in the wet lab to move beyond a limited set of players, this number of players is still significantly larger than in traditional wet-lab science. In addition, although this has not yet happened, it is certainly possible that annotation of the data generated by a wet-lab collaboration could invoke the DAS model and thus encompass a much larger group.

For collaborative projects, the gains that can accrue from disavowal of intellectual property rights are significant. Unlike the AFCS, universities and investigators involved in other large-scale collaborative projects funded by the NIGMS have not similarly disavowed such rights. Without disavowal of intellectual property rights, concerns that information exchange will lead to public disclosure of proprietary information, as well as disputes over how to allocate patent rights among a host of potential university assignees, may create friction. The principal investigator of one consortium that has not disavowed proprietary rights, Alan Horwitz of the Cell Migration Consortium, reports some dissatisfaction with the manner in which the relevant university TTOs in his consortium conducted their negotiations. He believes that TTO-imposed requirements whereby each university agrees to keep strictly confidential and refrain from commercializing the proprietary information of other universities in the consortium have "gotten in the way of the science."[76] Horwitz hopes that the relevant interuniversity agreements will be renegotiated in the future. The possibility that better agreements will be produced in the future is not necessarily high, however. Within wet-lab biomedical research, universities jealously guard their ability to commercialize proprietary information, particularly by turning it into patents. To turn proprietary information into patents, strict restrictions on dissemination are necessary: The relevant court decisions by the Federal Circuit hold that even limited public sharing of information can create patent-defeating prior art.[77] The prevailing regime governing exploitation rules for patents also makes collaborative research difficult. For example, each inventor or assignee to whom the right has been assigned can fully exploit the patent and there is no duty to account. As Rochelle Dreyfuss has noted, "The result of these exploitation rules is a rivalry that is potentially so destructive [that] the need to consolidate rights in a single owner is overwhelming."[78]

The disavowal of intellectual property rights in wet-lab biology raises concerns about commercialization. It is certainly possible that some of the information placed in the public domain by projects like the AFCS will be left to linger in an undeveloped state, as feared by the proponents of Bayh-Dole. At least in the specific context of the AFCS, however, the fact that pharmaceutical companies fund some of the research indicates that commercialization is unlikely to be altogether defeated. More generally, the evidence that public domain status for upstream information defeats commercialization is hardly solid. What public domain status for such information may do is undermine some small biotechnology firms. However, small biotechnology firms are unlikely to have the resources necessary to conduct large-scale systems biology experiments.

As an institutional matter, if projects like the AFCS are going to work, either their publication model or the print publication emphasis of the biological sciences may need modification. As matters currently stand, the lack of emphasis on print publication, coupled with the disavowal of patents, has meant that only the AFCS lab heads are traditional academics. To the extent that complex systems biology projects will succeed only if they attract the most academically oriented young minds, the failure to attract such researchers is worrisome. It is important, therefore, that the AFCS appear to be moving toward more conventional publication for its own investigators. It is also important that the AFCS is explicitly encouraging other investigators to use its data as the basis for publication in peer-reviewed journals. As noted earlier, a statement by prestigious peer-reviewed publications making it clear they do not discriminate against articles based on data already made publicly available would be useful. In the long term, a move in the biological sciences toward a model that emphasizes (or at least recognizes) Web-based publication, with subsequent peer review, is also worth considering.

From an institutional standpoint, it is also worth noting that university agreements to disavow intellectual property rights are not easy to achieve. Only charismatic and superbly credentialed scientists like Al Gilman are likely to secure such agreements. They do so by convincing their scientific colleagues that they must sign on to a particular research project, whatever the political difficulties. Moreover, even individuals like Gilman probably have to be supported by the relevant funding agency.

Given these institutional obstacles, one might reasonably ask whether the large-scale collaborative work necessary for systems biology needs to be done using consortia of the type represented by the AFCS. Rather, a large pharmaceutical firm might be the appropriate arena for such work. One might imagine, for example, that Pfizer could set up eight laboratories like the AFCS laboratories. To guard against the innovation-suppressing tendencies of large hierarchies, these laboratories could also be given substantial freedom to pursue the projects that they want to pursue. A Pfizer-based collaborative project would not have to worry about allocating intellectual property rights. Moreover, given that all work is done within a single firm, it is unlikely that even robust exchange of information within the firm would be deemed public, so as to create patent-defeating prior art.

Interestingly, there is some movement in the pharmaceutical industry toward large-scale collaboration. However, the collaboration contemplated is not within the firm but *between* firms. An organization called the CEO Roundtable on Cancer is considering a proposal to create a research collaboration among a large number of companies for purposes of making an "all-out effort against cancer." Various pharmaceutical firms are considering this collaboration between firms, even though the obstacles related to allocation of intellectual property rights—not to mention antitrust concerns—are quite considerable.[79] The cost to a single company of doing such systems biology research may be sufficiently great or the possibility of attaching intellectual property rights that recoup the cost sufficiently small that no single company wants to engage in the research. In that case, the research may be better produced as a public good, as by the AFCS.

Conclusion

Approaches to biomedical research in which such research is generated and improved upon in an open, collaborative fashion represent a potentially valuable experiment. The most intuitive case for such an experiment is open source bioinformatics software. In the case of software, the major obstacle to successful experimentation could be removed by instituting contractual mechanisms to divide consulting revenues between investigators and universities. With respect to open and collaborative databases, the argument is somewhat more equivocal. Nonetheless, when the data in question are upstream, a significant case can be made in favor of publicly funded, publicly available databases that can be improved on collaboratively. The case becomes weaker as the information being produced is downstream in the research path. Rather than using copyleft style licensing that undermines patents on downstream information, it may be advisable to attract collaborators by attempting to change biological science norms regarding publication. Such norm change would also improve the value of experimentation with large-scale collaboration in wet-lab systems biology. In particular, it would help such collaborations to attract promising young investigators. Although open and collaborative research represents a paradigm shift for wet-lab biology, experimentation with such a paradigm shift might be necessary for solving the intractable biological problems that are currently impeding the development of breakthrough drugs. Moreover, to the extent that large-scale wet-lab collaborations that disavow upstream intellectual property rights can find pharmaceutical company support, they are unlikely to undermine critical patents.

Notes

1. See, e.g., John P. Walsh, Ashish Arora, and Wesley M. Cohen, "Effects of Research Tool Patents and Licensing on Biomedical Innovation," in *Patents in the Knowledge-Based Economy*, ed. Wesley M. Cohen and Stephen A. Merrill (Washington, D.C.: National Academies Press, 2003), 285 (discussing increased concentration of proprietary rights in upstream biomedical research).

2. See, e.g., Eric G. Campbell et al., "Data Withholding in Academic Genetics: Data from a National Survey," *JAMA* 287 (2002): 473; John Walsh and Wei Hong, "Secrecy Is Increasing in Step with Competition," *Nature* 422 (2003): 801 (empirical findings indicating increased secrecy in biomedical research). I discuss the extent to which increases in proprietary rights and secrecy appear to be correlated later in the chapter.

3. For examples of such calls for access, see, e.g., National Research Council, *Sharing Publication-related Data and Materials: Responsibilities of Authorship in the Life Sciences* (Washington, D.C.: National Academies Press, 2003); Department of Health and Human Services, National Institutes of Health, "Principles and Guidelines for Recipients of NIH Research Grants and Contracts on Obtaining and Disseminating Biomedical Research Resources: Final Notice," *Federal Register* 64 (December 23, 1999): 72,090, 72,093 (research tools).

4. The term *open and collaborative projects* was recently invoked in a letter to the World Intellectual Property Organization (WIPO) urging WIPO to hold an exploratory meeting on these types of projects. See "Letter from Sixty-eight Scientists and Economists to Kamil Idris, Director General of the World Intellectual Property Organization, July 7, 2003," available at www.cptech.org/ip/wipo/kamil-idris-7July2003.pdf. That letter does not specifically define its use of the term. This chapter's definition is set out in the text.

5. See, e.g., William Jorgensen, "The Many Roles of Computation in Drug Discovery," *Science* 303 (2004): 1818.

6. See International HapMap Project Public Access License, available at www.hapmap.org/cgi-perl/registration (acknowledging model of GNU General Public License).

7. See, e.g., Dan Burk, "Open Source Genomics," *Boston University Journal of Science and Technology* 8 (2002): 254, 255. For a preliminary empirical investigation in the journalistic literature, see Kenneth Neil Cukier, "Community Property: Open-Source Proponents Plant the Seeds of New Landscape," *Acumen* 1 (2003): 57–58.

8. For purposes of this paper, I focus on research that addresses diseases prevalent in developed countries and assume (somewhat heroically) that market demand accurately reflects the socially desirable direction and rate of innovation.

9. Caitlin Smith, "A Question of Biology," *Nature* 428 (2004): 225, 231 (noting comment by scientist that "[i]n the past, a simplistic view was, by necessity, taken,

which resulted in many drugs failing in preclinical or clinical trials for lack of efficacy or side effects. The new approach must account for this complexity. The holistic systems biology approach to research will be necessary to overcome this challenge.").

10. Iain M. Cockburn, "The Changing Structure of the Pharmaceutical Industry," *Health Affairs* 23 (2004): 10, 11; Robert F. Service, "Surviving the Blockbuster Syndrome," *Science* 303 (2004): 1796 (discussing low number of new chemical entities approved in 2002).

11. See, e.g., Wesley Cohen et al., "Protecting their Intellectual Assets: Appropriability Conditions and Why U.S. Manufacturing Firms Patent (or Not)" (working paper no. 7552, NBER, Cambridge, Mass., 2000).

12. Compare Robert K. Merton, "The Normative Structure of Science," in *The Sociology of Science* (Chicago: University of Chicago Press, 1973) (famously arguing that, in general, academic research science is a communal enterprise).

13. Walsh and Hong, "Secrecy Is Increasing." Cited in note 2.

14. See, e.g., Arti K. Rai, "Regulating Scientific Research: Intellectual Property Rights and the Norms of Science," *Northwestern Law Review* 94 (1999): 77, 92.

15. The view of patents enunciated in Bayh-Dole is closely associated with those scholars who view patents as directly analogous to rights in tangible property. Like the grant of rights in tangible property, an early decision to grant patent rights ensures that the subject of the right is developed or utilized at the appropriate rate, neither "too fast" nor "too slow." See Edmund Kitch, "The Nature and Function of the Patent System," *Journal of Law and Economics* 20 (1977): 265 (applying property rights theory enunciated by Harold Demsetz to patents and discussing how an early grant of rights can guard against both "racing" and underdevelopment).

16. See, e.g., *In re Brana*, 53 F.3d 1560 (Fed.Cir. 1995) (utility); *In re Deuel*, 51 F.3d 1552 (Fed. Cir. 1995) (nonobviousness).

17. International Patent Classification categories, coupled with data on all university patents, can provide some rough sense of the university patent presence in biomedical research. In 2000, the percentage of biomedical research patents secured by research universities was somewhere between 11 percent (using a "liberal" definition of biomedical research that may sweep in some patents on end products) to 15 percent (using a more "conservative" definition of biomedical research). This compares with a university percentage of between 2 to 5 percent in 1980. Thanks to Bhaven Sampat (assistant professor, School of Public Policy, Georgia Institute of Technology) for this data.

18. See, e.g., *University of Rochester v. G. D. Searle*, 358 F.2d 916 (2004); *Regents of the Univ. of Cal. v. Eli Lilly*, 119 F.3d 1559 (Fed. Cir. 1997) (striking down broad patents on biomedical research).

19. *Amgen v. Hoechst Marion Roussel, Inc.*, 314 F.3d 1313 (upholding broad biomedical patent).

20. Empirical evidence regarding the superior innovative capacities of small firms is mixed, however. See Zoltan J. Acs and David B. Audretsch, "Innovation in

Large and Small Firms: An Empirical Analysis," *American Economic Review* 78 (1988): 678 (finding that in twenty-one of thirty-five industries, large firms were more innovative than small firms).

21. Ronald Coase, "A Theory of the Firm," *Economica* 4 (1937): 386.

22. Walsh, Arora, and Cohen, "Effects of Research Tool Patents." Cited in note 1.

23. Ibid.; see also Josh Lerner, "Patenting in the Shadow of Competitors," *Journal of Law and Economics* 38 (1995): 463.

24. *Rochester v. Searle; Ariad v. Eli Lilly.*

25. Campbell et al., "Data Withholding." Cited in note 2. Thirty-five percent of geneticists said that sharing had decreased during the 1990s, whereas only 14 percent said that sharing had increased.

26. See 35 U.S.C. 102(b) (establishing that an invention cannot be patented if it has been disclosed publicly more than one year before a patent application is filed).

27. See David Blumenthal et al., "Withholding Research Results in Academic Life Science," *JAMA* 277 (1997): 1224.

28. Campbell et al., "Data Withholding." Cited in note 2.

29. Ibid. Cf. John P. Walsh, "For Money or Glory? Secrecy, Competition, and Commercialization in Science" (presentation at American Sociological Association Annual Meeting, August 16, 2004) (finding increased secrecy but determining it was not associated with a patent application).

30. Cf. Elinor Ostrom, *Governing the Commons* (Cambridge: Cambridge University Press, 1990), 88–89 (noting that enduring norms operate where the group is small and has similar interests and values).

31. Bruce Perens, "The Open Source Definition," available at http://perens.com/articles/osd.html.

32. Although Richard Stallman and some others argue that copylefted software should be called free software, this paper uses the term *open source* to encompass copylefted software.

33. Jonathan Zittrain, "Evaluating Free and Proprietary Software," *University of Chicago Law Review* 71 (2004): 265, 279. According to Josh Lerner and Jean Tirole, approximately 70 percent of the 25,729 projects found at www.sourceforge.net used GPL-style licenses. Joshua Lerner and Jean Tirole, "The Scope of Open Source Licensing," (Harvard NOM working paper no. 02-42, 2002), available at http://papers.ssrn.com/sol3/papers.cfm?abstract_id=354220.

34. Discussion at American Bar Association, Joint Session of Intellectual Property Section and Science and Technology Section, April 1, 2004. There are two recorded instances of litigation brought by holders of copyleft licenses claiming improper propertization of the code. Zittrain, "Evaluating Free and Proprietary Software," 285. Cited in note 33.

35. S. O'Mahony, "Guarding the Commons: How Community Managed Projects Protect Their Work," *Research Policy* 32 (2003): 1179, 1189.

36. See generally Eric von Hippel and Georg von Krogh, "Editorial, Special Issue of Open Source Software Development," *Research Policy* 32 (2003): 1149. The central developers' control of the project is sufficiently high that "forking" of the source code is rare. Eric Raymond, "The Magic Cauldron," sections 3–5, available at http://www.catb.org/~ESR/writings/magic-cauldron/magic-cauldron.html.

37. Compare David McGowan, "Legal Implications of Open-Source Software," *University of Illinois Law Review* (2001): 241 (discussing respects in which open source software production is and is not like firm-based production).

38. According to one survey, only about 7 percent of open source software developers work in the academic sector. Karim R. Lakhani and Robert G. Wolf, "Why Hackers Do What They Do: Understanding Motivation Effort in Free/Open Source Software Projects," in *Perspectives on Free and Open Source Software,* ed. J. Feller, B. Fitzgerald, S. Hissam, and K. R. Lakhani (Cambridge, Mass.: MIT Press, 2005).

39. See, generally, ibid.; see also Lerner and Tirole, "Scope of Open Source Licensing." Cited in note 33.

40. James W. Paulson et al., "An Empirical Study of Open-Source and Closed-Source Software Products," *IEEE Transactions on Software Engineering* SE-30 (2004): 246.

41. For firms that use software platforms, the cost of the software may be only a small part of the total cost of ownership. In particular, staffing costs for such platforms can be quite high. See Alan MacCormack, "Evaluating Total Cost of Ownership for Software Platforms: Comparing Apples, Oranges, and Cucumbers," available at http://www.aei.brookings.org/admin/authorpdfs/page.php?id=261. Staffing costs are likely to be less important, however, where the software in question is itself directed at a technical audience (as is most bioinformatics software).

42. Yochai Benkler, "Coase's Penguin, or Linux and the Nature of the Firm," *Yale Law Journal* 112 (2002): 369.

43. Interview with computational biologist Steven Brenner, UC Berkeley, March 13, 2004. According to the founding developers of Bioperl, "[a] primary motivation behind writing the toolkit is the authors' desire to focus energies on a solution whose components can be shared rather than duplicating effort." Jason E. Stajich et al., "The Bioperl Toolkit: Perl Modules for the Life Sciences," *Genome Research* 12 (2002): 1611.

44. Ibid. See also Russ Altman et al., "Whitepaper on Open Source Software in Bioinformatics," available at https://www.iscb.org/lists/iscb-software.html/dir/msg0000.shtml (on file with author) (arguing that NIH should not mandate open source for its grant recipients).

45. See Arti Rai, "Open and Collaborative Biomedical Research: An Empirical Look" (draft paper, on file with author) (discussing policies of twenty research universities with large software patent, biomedical patent, and/or biomedical research portfolios).

46. Ibid.

47. University representations are borne out by the numbers. One estimate based on International Patent Classifications (IPCs) common for software publishing industry patents indicates that universities actually patented less as a relative matter in 2000 than they did in 1980. While university software patents represented 1 percent of all software in 1980, they represented 0.6 percent of all such patents in 2000. Thanks to Bhaven Sampat for data on software patents.

48. Rai, "Open and Collaborative Biomedical Research." Cited in note 45.

49. Ibid.

50. Interviews with Lita Nelsen (director, Technology Licensing Office, MIT) and Kathy Ku (director, Stanford Office of Technology and Licensing), September 5, 2003.

51. Interview with Georgia Harper (manager, Intellectual Property Section, University of Texas Office of General Counsel), February 5, 2003.

52. In January 2003, NHGRI extended this policy of immediate data deposition without accompanying intellectual property rights to all large-scale data "infrastructure" projects. Indeed, at this meeting, NHGRI gave higher priority to immediate and full access to data than to the traditional scientific norm that the investigator who generates the data has the right to do the first analysis of this data. *Nature* 421 (2003): 875.

53. Interview with Lincoln Stein, March 26, 2004.

54. See Eliot Marshall, "Genome Researchers Take the Pledge: Data Sharing," *Science*, April 26, 1996, 478 (noting that key university patent officials approved of policy). One leading officer, Lita Nelsen of MIT, noted, however, that she is wary of the "bad precedent" that the policy might set. Ibid.

55. John Sulston, *The Common Thread* (Washington, D.C.: Joseph Henry Press, 2002), 211.

56. Similarly, another important open and collaborative project that took place at approximately the same time as the HGP, the Single Nucleotide Polymorphism (SNP) Consortium, put its data in the public domain.

57. See International HapMap Project Public Access License, available at www.hapmap.org/cgi-perl/registration.

58. Because there is no underlying copyright, those who manage to access the data without having agreed to the license are not subject to any legal prohibition against patenting. The relative weakness of the HapMap prohibition is probably salutary, however, because, as discussed later in the chapter, a direct application of copyleft licensing for biological databases may impede commercialization unduly. On December 10, 2004, as this chapter was going to press, the leaders of the HapMap project announced that license restrictions had been lifted because haplotype information was now available.

59. The creation of genome sequence databases also has a wet-lab component. The wet-lab component was particularly substantial before the widespread dissemination of automated laser-based sequencing machines. But the wet-lab component is small and relatively easy to standardize, at least as compared to traditional biology.

60. Interview with Al Gilman, September 4, 2003.

61. Interview with Shankar Subramanian (professor of bioengineering, UCSD), March 17, 2004.

62. See www.signaling-gateway.org/data/Protocol/Links.html.

63. Interview with Alex Brown (Ingram Associate Professor of Cancer Research, Vanderbilt University), April 23, 2004.

64. See www.signaling-gateway.org/data/Data.html (AFCS data center, hosted by AFCS and *Nature*).

65. See www.signaling-gateway.org/reports/ReportCover.html.

66. Interview with Alex Brown, March 16, 2004. Brown notes that most data, including the data generated by the AFCS, are not as publicly visible, as were the data from the Human Genome Project.

67. See www.signaling-gateway.org/reports/JournalPubs.htm.

68. Interview with Alex Brown, April 23, 2004.

69. Interview with Al Gilman, September 4, 2003.

70. More generally, the role played by patents in the software industry is unclear. In contrast, drug patents, and perhaps even patents on certain types of upstream work, are clearly important to the biopharmaceutical industry.

71. Memorandum from Pat Jones (director, Office of Technology Transfer, University of Arizona) discussing cases, March 2004.

72. One concern that has recently emerged is the possibility of contributors to open source adding code that may have property rights attached to it. Because it is very difficult for open source project leaders to verify that contributors are adding code that is free of proprietary rights, the *SCO v. IBM* lawsuit, in which SCO claims copyright interests over parts of UNIX that have allegedly been incorporated into Linux, has generated much concern in the open source community. At this early stage, however, the potential implications of this lawsuit, particularly for university-based open source researchers, are difficult to gauge.

73. James Shreeve, *Genome Wars* (New York: Knopf, 2004), 368–69.

74. See supra note 34.

75. This model has been used successfully, for example, in other natural sciences, primarily physics. See www.arXiv.org.

76. Interview with Alan Horwitz, March 31, 2004.

77. The recently enacted Cooperative Research and Technology Enhancement Act of 2004 (CREATE) aims to encourage collaborations by reducing the likelihood that so-called secret prior art created by the collaboration will defeat patentability. But this law does not address public disclosure of prior art created by the collaboration.

78. Rochelle Dreyfuss, "Collaborative Research: Conflicts on Authorship, Ownership, and Accountability," *Vanderbilt Law Review* 53 (2000): 1161.

79. Susan Warner, "Collaborators against Cancer," *Scientist,* June 30, 2003 (noting these obstacles).

7

Does Open Source Have Legs?

Wesley M. Cohen

The "open source" model of innovation is a vehicle for freely disseminating the fruits of software development to end users, as well as across those engaged in the development process itself. This latter feature is argued to make the open source model effective in advancing technology and is the focus of this chapter.

Recently, some have proposed that the open source model might apply to other research domains, notably biomedical innovation. I consider this possibility in the paper by briefly addressing two questions that should be entertained, no matter the prospective application area. First, what features of the open source model permitted it to emerge in some areas of software development, and might we find at least some of those conditions in other innovation-intensive settings, particularly biomedicine? Second, is society better off by applying this model to biomedicine or any other domain?

Background

Before addressing these questions, we need to briefly characterize what we mean by the "open source" model of innovation, especially as it might apply outside of software. First, in software, the "source code" encompasses the set of underlying programming instructions that provide the skeleton on which applications are hung; and in those areas where software is developed on a proprietary rather than open source basis, the source code is not distributed

I gratefully acknowledge the helpful comments of Bob Hahn and Arti Rai.

with an application, potentially impeding the ability of downstream developers to modify or improve it. For other technologies, one might think of the analogue to "source code" as R & D inputs, including data, software, or prior discoveries, that are essential to follow-on applications, improvements, or further discoveries. The distinctive feature of the "open source" model of innovation is that a given piece of software is made broadly and freely available in its entirety (i.e., including the source code) to anyone who might wish to modify it or build on it, often with the understanding that his own work would then be subject to the same condition. Thus, there is often the understanding, sometimes formally implemented, of some degree of reciprocal free access to the fruits of creative labor: that no one would take what is freely available as an input into his own R & D efforts and then assert exclusivity over the work that builds on that input. The other feature of this model is that subsequent improvements and refinements typically occur on a distributed, decentralized basis, permitting self-selected individuals to contribute improvements and critical scrutiny to the effort.

Before considering whether open source may be an appropriate model for fostering innovation, we need to acknowledge that open source is a particular way of promoting R & D–related information flows across individuals and firms and such flows, even across direct rivals, are common, although rarely structured in the way open source is. When considered in the context of firms, it is understood that such R & D–related information flows yield offsetting effects for an industry's rate of technical advance. First, to the degree that either the informational inputs or outputs of a firm's R & D activities flow freely to rival firms, the less the R & D–performing firm is able to appropriate the returns to its R & D effort and the lower is the incentive to invest in R & D to begin with. Considered at the level of the industry as a whole, these same information flows, however, can increase the productivity of each firm's R & D, and thus stimulate technical advance. These flows can substitute for a firm's R & D if, for example, they spare the firm from undertaking what would otherwise be duplicative effort, yielding what Spence calls an "efficiency" effect.[1] Alternatively, these flows may complement the firm's ongoing R & D, by suggesting, for example, fruitful new approaches to a problem or even altogether new projects.[2] In either event, these flows make the R & D activities of the firms within an industry more productive. Thus, at the level of an industry or a technology, R & D–related information flows pose a tradeoff for technical advance. Their negative appropriability incentive effect tends to offset the complementarity or efficiency effects that allows firms to achieve greater technical advance (per unit of effort).

Thus, although R & D-related information flows across rivals offer the promise of making each firm's R & D more productive, they also undermine the incentive to undertake that R & D to begin with. The policy challenge, however, is that there is no reason to believe that market incentives will lead to an optimal level of information flow from a social welfare perspective.[3] Indeed, from any individual firm's perspective, there is little or no tradeoff. Despite the benefits that might accrue to each firm from participating in a richer information environment (i.e., one in which there are more R & D information flows), firms rarely see it in their interest to contribute to these flows. First, firms do not typically believe that information outflow is tied to inflow.[4] Indeed, the preponderance of R & D information flows across rivals are unintended, and the private incentive of each firm is to reduce outflows as much as possible. Second, even if firms had some sense that the richness of the broader information environment depended on each firm's contributing some information, it would still be in each firm's interest to free ride; the broader information environment would still suffer from the conventional collective action dilemma characterizing the provision of a public good. Although firms may even believe that they are collectively better off with more information flow, it is in no one firm's interest to contribute to those flows.

Thus, market incentives favor stronger appropriation and suppression of R & D–related information outflows. The likelihood that innovating firms will try to appropriate as large a share as possible of the returns to an innovation without disclosing any of the details, to the possible detriment of technical advance more generally, is recognized, for example, in patent policy. In exchange for a legal sanction to exclude others from using one's invention, a patent holder is required to disclose publicly details of the protected invention. On rare occasions, the federal government, motivated by antitrust concerns, intervenes to induce an innovating firm to provide other firms access to a key invention that is essential to follow-on research and development. For example, over forty years ago, the U.S. government forced AT&T to license widely its fundamental patent for transistor technology on liberal terms, fostering the creation of the semiconductor industry. In some cases, firms themselves recognize the benefits of locating in information-rich environments, even at some cost to their ability to appropriate rents from their R & D. Gilson, for example, highlights Novartis' decision to locate a major R & D facility in the Bay area, notwithstanding the unenforceability of noncompete clauses in employment contracts in California.[5] Gilson suggests that Novartis made this decision because it knew that all other firms in the state had to operate under the same terms and expected that the rich information flows available there would more than offset any possible advantages gained by rivals from Novartis' R & D spillovers.[6]

Open Source and the Tradeoffs Associated with R & D Information Flows

From the vantage point of the conventional tradeoffs associated with R & D information flows, the open source model of innovation breaks the mold. As typically implemented, those who invest effort in open source innovation are willing to permit the fruits of their labor to be freely used, modified, and improved by others. In this case, R & D information flows seemingly do not come at the expense of the incentive to put forth creative effort. Why not?

First, much open source development is realized through the effort of individuals acting on their own behalf. Despite a lack of consensus on why these individuals do what they do, there is agreement that their incentives are not pecuniary, at least not in the short run. Some suggest that their incentives are nonetheless extrinsic, associated with reputation and employment prospects,[7] while others provide evidence that the incentives are more intrinsic, associated with the pleasure of creating or the satisfaction that comes from contributing to a community endeavor.[8] In either case, however, these individual contributors do not seek to restrict access to the fruits of their labor and, indeed, may even derive utility from sharing their work with others. The nonpecuniary motives of these individuals imply, at least in the context of open source, a reconception of the appropriability incentive associated with innovative effort to reflect the possibility that contributors may derive pleasure and benefit from others' freely using their ideas. Under such circumstances, contributors appropriate more (nonpecuniary) benefit the more their work is freely used by others.

Therefore, for many individuals who freely contribute to software development, the conventional tradeoff between the appropriability and R & D productivity effects characterizing R & D–related information flows does not apply. Not only does the appropriability incentive effect not conflict with the complementarity and efficiency effects of information flows, but the two effects may reinforce one another, especially if, for example, the size of the community to which each individual contributes plays a role in affecting perceived benefits. In this case, we may have a "virtuous cycle" of positive, self-reinforcing feedback between the appropriability and complementarity/efficiency effects of information flows, and this self-reinforcement itself may spawn self-propagating behavior through which the open source model may then diffuse.

One might think that only individuals may thrive in an open source environment because they can respond to nonpecuniary goals; they do not live or die on the basis of financial returns, as do firms. Firms, however, can also operate, wholly or partially, in open source software development environments. Consider, for example, Red Hat, the leading corporate marketer and provider of services for the Linux operating system. The obvious question is how a firm like Red Hat makes its money if it does not rely on intellectual property protection in the form of either patents or copyrights. The first thing to understand is that, in numerous industries, firms do not protect their innovations chiefly through legal mechanisms such as patents, but rather through the use of secrecy, lead time advantage, or capabilities, such as marketing, sales, or manufacturing, that complement their innovations.[9] Although there are no systematic data on how firms protect software innovation, it is likely that, in some software markets, firms may be able to profit from software innovation without relying principally on legal protection assuring exclusive access. Red Hat, for example, makes its money principally by bundling its version of the Linux operating system with distinctive service and support for the product.[10] More generally, Red Hat's business model reflects a symbiosis between individuals who contribute to product development for free, and firms like Red Hat that manage to profit from the work of these individuals without restricting access to the software code they promote.[11] Thus, the source of Red Hat's rents is not exclusive access to code but a distinctive ability to combine and coordinate the code developed by others, market it, provide support, and brand it without having to compromise the principles of the open source model of innovation. This means of profiting from innovation also implies that, in some markets, even where open source code is "viral,"[12] software firms may still be able to profit from downstream innovation and commercialization with strategies that do not turn critically on either copyright or patent protection.

Why Else in Software?

Thus far, we have suggested that open source works in software domains where free access and appropriability incentives complement rather than offset one another in stimulating individuals to freely contribute to the broader effort. There are additional reasons why open source has become a popular approach to software development in selected domains.

Open source software development reflects a bottom-up, decentralized process, and appears to have emerged at least partly because product development is modular and low cost. Given its modular character, it benefits from the input of many, without need for direct coordination across contributors. The low cost of software development means that there is little financial barrier to participate in its development. It is low cost partly because the requisite equipment is modest. Consequently, contributors require little other than their own skill, prior training, and ingenuity. It is also low cost because the main opportunity cost comes either in the form of a sacrifice of individual contributors' leisure time or at the cost to employers of time spent by employees on open source projects in lieu of work.[13] In other words, the overall endeavor is low cost partly because the individuals involved tend to have independent means of support—"day jobs" in academia or industry. While surely the emergence of the open source model is abetted by norms of mutuality and individual achievement, we suggest, therefore, it is also supported by circumstances that impose modest financial demands on individual contributors and hence little need to support the endeavor out of the returns to the activity itself. If, in contrast, this activity required substantial investment expenditure, then, absent a subsidy, we conjecture that some form of private gain—and the exclusive access required to achieve it—would then become more essential.

A requirement of little or no contributor investment may not be sufficient, however, for open source to flourish. Even where financial requirements are modest, an expectation of significant benefit from some form of restricted access to the fruits of individuals' labor may be sufficient to push potential contributors away from the norms of open source. One might suggest, however, that in those domains of software where open source thrives, the contribution of no one or even several individuals is typically commercializable. Rather, value rides on the labor of the many whose contributions need to work in combination. Therefore, another condition that would tend to foster the emergence of an open source environment is that there is a perceived advantage in combining the effort of many. While organizing such an effort is within the purview of larger firms, from any one individual's perspective there are barriers to organizing the work of a distributed network and, more important, barriers to any one individual effectively restricting the access to the work of such a distributed network in a way that would yield a commercial return.

On the basis of the discussion thus far, we can identify conditions that, if not essential to the success of the open source model, at least appear to have advanced its acceptance and use in selected domains of software development:

1. Nonpecuniary incentives on the part of individual contributors impart little motive to restrict access to the fruits of their labor.

2. The sharing of innovation-related information increases individual contributors' utility.

3. The potential exists for complementarities and efficiencies in R & D activities across contributors and firms.

4. Contributions can be made at low cost or are subsidized.

5. An extensive network of capable contributors exists.

6. The product and product development process are modular.

7. Firms potentially involved with the commercial development and promotion of open source products can protect the competitive advantage associated with those products using means other than intellectual property rights.

Can Open Source Methods Be Applied to Biomedical Research?

To consider whether an open source model might work in biomedicine or in any other area of innovation, we should consider the nature of the incentives of the individuals and firms concerned, as well as the costs and benefits that would accrue. The preceding discussion of the experience of open source methods in software provides some insight into the range of factors that might apply to this sort of analysis. An analysis of all these factors in biomedicine, however, extends beyond the scope of the current paper. Indeed, if one were to conduct such an ambitious study, we would first, following Rai's contribution to this volume, want to break down the relevant domains of biomedical research into software, databases, and wet-lab research. I, however, frame much of my discussion in terms of "wet-lab work," as opposed to data or software development. I focus on the individuals or organizations that do the R & D, their incentives, and the extent to which these incentives build on exclusive access to either inputs into their research or the output of that research.

To consider these issues for biomedicine, I coarsely distinguish between those individuals (including academics) and firms concerned largely with upstream research, and those firms concerned with the more downstream development of drugs, other therapeutics, and diagnostic tools that are also responsible for commercialization. An important feature of biomedical innovation is that an active market for technology, built largely on the strength of patent protection, permits upstream researchers and firms to sell disembodied innovations and research tools to downstream firms.[14]

The downstream pharmaceutical firms that commercialize drugs and other therapeutics earn their return to their substantial R & D expenditures by combining patent protection with strong distribution and marketing capabilities. The pharmaceutical industry is unusual among manufacturing industries in the degree to which its business model relies on patent rights as a key source of rents.[15] Given the importance of patent rights to this business model, these firms are not about to eschew those rights to embrace anything resembling an open source model. In turn, they are reluctant to exploit any inputs into their research process that would require them to disavow such rights. Therefore, for open source to have any opportunity to succeed even in upstream domains of biomedical research, pharmaceutical firms must know that such use would not compromise their ability to profit from the compounds and other products they develop using those inputs. This implies that "open source" methods could not be adopted in the viral form that requires users of open source products to adopt the open source conventions of free and open access.

Does the importance of patents for the commercialization of drugs and other therapeutics necessarily imply, therefore, that firms and individuals who work on upstream biomedical innovations are unlikely to adopt open source conventions? Not necessarily. Large pharmaceutical firms prefer to have free access to upstream discoveries for use in their own research, as long as that free access does not constrain their ability to use patents to protect the drugs that they themselves develop. However, the extent to which large pharmaceutical firms are the consumers of such upstream research certainly acts as a brake on the adoption of the viral form of the open source model.

Even, however, where intellectual property (IP)–based development and commercialization are not a concern to upstream researchers, the conventions of the open source model may still not be embraced among academics and others doing the upstream research. Historically, researchers in biomedicine (and in every other field) have long built on one another's discoveries as a matter of course. At the same time, of course, there was scientific competition and, to varying degrees, the secrecy that attends upon such competition. So, while there was openness and the ability to build upon one another's work with respect to published outcomes, access to constructed databases and more intermediate findings could be quite restricted. Indeed, in their history of the Human Genome Project, Sulston and Ferry note the different traditions with regard to openness between the human geneticists, who jealously guarded their data, versus researchers working on decoding the genetic sequence of the nematode worm (*c. elegans*) who would publicly disclose their findings and their data in the course of their work.[16] Thus, even in academic biomedical research, there are and remain different norms regarding openness; and clearly the conventions of open source, particularly as applied to data and intermediate findings, may not be embraced by all, even in the absence of commercial considerations. Thus, contrary to norms of mutuality characterizing many of those who work in software as well as in some domains of genomic research, some researchers, possibly entire subfields, respond to the pressures of scientific competition by restricting access to data and other information related to their ongoing work.

An important empirical question, therefore, is how pervasive and powerful are these norms of scientific competition built around priority of discovery? Notwithstanding the dominance of the convention of free disclosure for the work produced by the Human Genome Project and related endeavors, the norms of secrecy and scientific competition remain pervasive. Indeed, Walsh and Hong found that, in a range of scientific fields, including experimental biology, secrecy has increased over the past forty years and the major predictor of secrecy is not patenting, nor even the expectation of gains from commercialization, but scientific competition.[17]

Perhaps the most important policy change affecting biomedical research since 1980 (other than the massive increase in government funding) is the Bayh-Dole Act, which granted institutions receiving federal research support the right to patent the findings of that research, much of which was upstream to the market. This meant that publishable findings might now serve two types of goals. In addition to satisfying researchers' nonpecuniary objectives (e.g., contributing to eminence, advancing knowledge), publishable findings offer the prospect of commercial gain from patent-protected discoveries via licensing, founding new firms, and the like, implying that pecuniary incentives may now supplement nonpecuniary incentives in the conduct of research. The particular challenge is that commercial gain associated with such research often depends heavily, and in some cases exclusively, on selling the information in disembodied form, which typically relies on some form of intellectual property protection. Thus, there is likely to be even greater pressure to restrict access to intermediate findings and data—using either intellectual property protection or secrecy—now that pecuniary incentives supplement the nonpecuniary ones long associated with scientific competition.[18]

Should Open Source Methods Be Applied to Biomedicine?

Prior to considering whether the biomedical community might embrace open source methods, one should consider whether it is worth trying. To address this question, we need some sense of the costs and benefits of such a regime shift. To probe that, it is important to understand the net social benefits of the current regime, where there is the option of filing for patent protection on upstream biomedical discoveries and research tools, as well as, of course, on downstream drugs, therapies, and diagnostics.

While it is clear that patents provide a powerful inducement to the downstream development and commercialization of drugs and other therapies,[19] one might be more skeptical about the net social benefits of patents for upstream biomedical research conducted in universities and nonprofit institutions. The private out-of-pocket costs of applying for a patent are reasonably well understood and not that high (although substantial enough—$10,000 to $30,000—to dissuade universities and other nonprofits from filing where the prospect of commercial gain is slight). However, the less tangible, potential social costs are of greater concern. Highlighted by Dasgupta and David, two such costs may include (1) impediments to subsequent research and innovation due to restricted access to a patented, upstream discovery and (2) possible reallocation of effort away from less commercially valuable, more-foundational research to more applied work with more apparent commercial value.[20] Evidence beyond anecdote and isolated illustration for either of these costs is, however, quite limited. In an interview-based study of the impact of the licensing and patenting of research tools on biomedical research, Walsh, Arora, and Cohen do not observe patents on upstream discoveries pervasively impeding research activity among academics and other researchers.[21] This study, however, was small in scale and awaits generalization. Regarding any prospective reallocation from more-foundational research to applied work, Breschi, Lissoni, and Montobbio, in a longitudinal study of 500 Italian professors, find no relationship between patenting and a shift in effort toward more applied research.[22] Perhaps more important, it is not even clear that such an allocational shift from upstream to more applied work would diminish social welfare in the long run. Calls for more "translational" research in biomedicine may even suggest, for example, that society is currently underinvesting in more applied research in biomedicine, although it is hard to know. Moreover, as Kline and Rosenberg suggest, in many fields, applied work often stimulates or guides upstream research.[23] Therefore, to place upstream research and more-downstream applied research and development in opposition oversimplifies the dynamics of the innovation process that propels technical advance. For our current purpose, the main point is that the critical social costs of the current intellectual property regime are not well understood.

Although IP protection on upstream biomedical discoveries may impose social costs, it may also confer important benefits. Chief among these are the incentive to undertake the R & D given the protection that IP rights may confer. Here, again, data are lacking. As noted previously, the findings of Arora, Ceccagnoli, and Cohen suggest that patenting strongly induces private sector, industrial R & D in pharmaceuticals, biotechnology, and medical devices.[24] No work, however, suggests whether the prospect of IP protection has any incentive effect on the level of academic and other noncommercial research in biomedicine or elsewhere. A priori, one would conjecture that, since such research is financed largely by public or philanthropic sources and the dominant motives, per the previous discussion, tend to be nonpecuniary, it is hard to believe that the prospect of patenting has much of an incentive effect on the level of effort. Even if IP protection, however, has relatively little impact on the conduct of public, upstream research, it at least appears to play a major role in spawning the numerous biotech ventures that provide a bridge between academic research and the downstream development and clinical testing required to bring drugs and therapies to market (cf. Henderson, Orsenigo, and Pisano[25]), yielding important social welfare benefits.

Alternatives

Let us suppose for the moment that society would benefit from greater access to upstream research than what is afforded under the current IP-based regime. What kind of intervention or institutional structure would achieve that? While promoting a form of the open source model may offer some advantages (assuming it is viable), its costs and benefits should be compared to other mechanisms, particularly if there are reasons to believe that an open source model may not be readily embraced. For example, there are numerous ways, some of them already implemented, in which the NIH or other funding sources could raise the cost of obtaining patent protection on upstream discoveries. Going even further than the current NIH guidelines bearing on the dissemination of data and research results, one could require (potentially contravening the Bayh-Dole Act) that such discoveries be made freely available for use by other researchers (even if patent protected) or risk denial of subsequent funding. In this or other ways, public agencies could simply elevate the private cost of restricting access to make the private costs of such more consistent with the social costs. Given that relatively few patented upstream discoveries yield significant returns (cf. Scherer and Harhoff[26]), the expected returns to such patenting and any associated restrictions on access are slight. Thus, for the preponderance of patentable discoveries, raising the more certain and immediate costs of actions to restrict access to such discoveries may provide a powerful disincentive to imposing restrictions on access. An alternative to raising costs is the possibility of creating a research exemption from liability for patent infringement for those using others' IP in noncommercial, upstream research. As discussed by the National Research Council, the crafting of such an exemption poses, however, a challenge.[27] Moreover, the research exemption would not address restrictions on access to upstream discoveries and data due to the use of secrecy as opposed to patents. The main point is that discussions of open source methods would benefit from a consideration of alternative mechanisms designed to encourage access to research, and any such consideration should grapple with not only the benefits for knowledge diffusion, but also the implications for the incentives to undertake the R & D to begin with.

Discussion

Given the broad range of unknowns highlighted with respect to the costs and benefits of the current regime and the various alternative models that might replace it, it is difficult to say whether an open source model should be promoted in lieu of the status quo or other alternative structures facilitating R & D information flow. One approach is to consider the issue for discrete, delineated research domains in biomedicine. Such a domain-specific approach may be advisable for addressing not only the normative but the positive question of whether open source or similar models of innovation are likely to be embraced by the scientists within an area. As noted, the norms and incentives that affect the diffusion of open source and related models vary even across subfields within biomedicine.

Recently, Maurer, Rai, and Sali implicitly adopted such a domain-specific approach in their proposal suggesting that open source methods could be fruitfully applied to upstream research bearing on tropical diseases, where there is relatively little commercial interest.[28] I agree with their implicit assessment that it may be especially challenging to implement open source methods in domains where significant commercial rewards are associated with the use of patents to exclude others from using your discoveries. Moreover, for tropical medicines, where commercial firms have shown little interest, one can say that an open source or related model does not sacrifice much in the way of research incentives, at least as applied to pharmaceutical firms. But, even in research on tropical medicine, there may be a motive to restrict access to data and intermediate findings; that is, scientific competition may matter. Accordingly, the question for biomedical research on tropical diseases is whether there is a prospect that individuals or individual labs can make the key breakthroughs on their own. If so, then the tradeoff we have considered may still apply, where what is being appropriated is not commercial reward but scientific eminence. If, on the other hand, the biomedical community recognizes that the underlying scientific challenges can best be addressed on the basis of more distributed contributions in this area, then perhaps open source methods can be fruitfully embraced. As noted at the outset of this chapter, it is important that we understand who or what is doing the work, and the nature of the incentives involved.

Notes

1. A. M. Spence, "Cost Reduction, Competition, and Industry Performance," *Econometrica* 52 (1984): 101–21.

2. R. C. Levin and P. Reiss, "Cost-Reducing and Demand-Creating R & D with Spillovers," *RAND Journal of Economics* 19 (1988): 538–56.

3. In this discussion, I assume that firms remain stand-alone. I do not consider the case where the prospect of internalizing complementarities or efficiencies in the research function motivates either strategic R & D alliances or mergers across firms. Such mergers or alliances, however, can be important vehicles for internalizing the benefits of what otherwise would be R & D spillovers.

4. As E. von Hippel, *The Sources of Innovation* (New York: Oxford University Press, 1988), observes, managers are often not cognizant of the reciprocal relationship inherent in such information flows across firms, even when their R & D employees commonly practice "tit-for-tat" information exchanges.

5. R. Gilson, "The Legal Infrastructure of High Technology Industrial Districts: Silicon Valley, Route 128 and Covenants Not to Compete," *New York University Law Review* 75 (1999).

6. Ibid.

7. J. Lerner and J. Tirole, "Some Simple Economics of Open Source," *Journal of Industrial Economics* 50, no. 2 (2002): 197–234; C. Fershtman and N. Gandal, "The Determinants of Output per Contributor in Open Source Projects: An Empirical Examination" (discussion paper no. 4329, CEPR [London], March 2004), http://ssrn.com/abstract=539783.

8. K. R. Lakhani and R. G. Wolf, "Why Hackers Do What They Do: Understanding Motivation and Effort in Free/Open Source Software Projects" (working paper no. 4425-03, MIT, Sloan School of Management, September 2003).

9. R. C. Levin, A. K. Klevorick, R. R. Nelson, and S. G. Winter, "Appropriating the Returns from Industrial R & D," *Brookings Papers on Economic Activity* (1987): 783–820; W. M. Cohen, R. R. Nelson, and J. P. Walsh, "Protecting Their Intellectual Assets: Appropriability Conditions and Why U.S. Manufacturing Firms Patent (or Not)" (working paper no. 7522, NBER, Cambridge, Mass., 2000; revised as mimeo, Duke University, 2004).

10. Red Hat, however, copyrights its support documentation and requires that if anyone modifies its version of Linux, the Red Hat name be stripped from the product.

11. Lerner and Tirole, "Some Simple Economics." Cited in note 7.

12. By viral, we mean those implementations of open source that require that who-ever improves the software in question will not, in turn, restrict access to the output of that work.

13. The time demands of the effort expended appear to be relatively modest (K. R. Lakhani and E. von Hippel, "How Open Source Software Works: Free User-to-User

Assistance," *Research Policy* 32 [2003]: 923–43), permitting these individuals to satisfy the obligations of their "day jobs."

14. Compare A. Arora, A. Fosfuri, and A. Gambardella, *Markets for Technology: The Economics of Innovation and Corporate Strategy* (Cambridge, Mass.: MIT Press, 2001).

15. Cohen, Nelson, and Walsh, "Protecting Their Intellectual Assets." Cited in note 9.

16. J. Sulston and G. Ferry, *The Common Thread* (Washington, D.C.: Joseph Henry Press, 2002).

17. J. P. Walsh and W. Hong, "Secrecy Is Increasing in Step with Competition," *Nature* 422 (2003): 801–2. In this volume, Rai describes the interesting case of the Alliance for Cell Signaling (AFCS), directed by Alfred Gilman of the University of Texas/Southwestern Medical School and funded by the National Institute of General Medical Science (NIGMS) of the NIH. Encouraged by the NIGMS, the AFCS adopted an aggressive posture toward disseminating its work. Rather than emphasizing the conventional channels of dissemination through scientific journals, the lab publishes findings on the Internet after an internal review. One possible consequence of this policy, however, is that many of the scientists who choose to work in this lab are not on a tenure track, perhaps suggesting that academic ventures that do not offer the conventional rewards of scientific credit and eminence may not attract the most academically oriented researchers.

18. Recall, however, that such restrictions on use and access may not, on balance, negatively affect social welfare to the extent that the incentives to conduct the research to begin with require such restrictions.

19. A. Arora, M. Ceccagnoli, and W. M. Cohen, "R & D and the Patent Premium" (mimeo, Carnegie Mellon University, 2004).

20. P. Dasgupta and P. A. David, "Towards a New Economics of Science," *Research Policy* 23 (1994): 487–521.

21. J. P. Walsh, A. Arora, and W. M. Cohen, "Effects of Research Tool Patents and Licensing on Biomedical Innovation," in *Patents in the Knowledge-Based Economy*, ed. W. Cohen and S. Merrill (Washington, D.C.: National Academies Press, 2003).

22. S. Breschi, F. Lissoni, and F. Montobbio, "Open Science and University Patenting: A Bibliometric Analysis of the Italian Case" (Tenth International J. A. Schumpeter Society Conference, Milan, Italy, June 9–12, 2004).

23. S. J. Kline and N. Rosenberg, "An Overview of Innovation," in *The Positive Sum Strategy: Harnessing Technology for Economic Growth*, ed. R. Landau and N. Rosenberg (Washington, D.C.: National Academies Press, 1986).

24. Arora, Ceccagnoli, and Cohen, "R & D and the Patent Premium." Cited in note 19.

25. R. Henderson, L. Orsenigo, and G. P. Pisano, "The Pharmaceutical Industry and the Revolution in Molecular Biology: Interactions among Scientific, Institutional and Organizational Change," in *Sources of Industrial Leadership: Studies of Seven Industries*, ed. D. C. Mowery and R. R. Nelson (New York: Cambridge University Press, 1999).

26. F. M. Scherer and D. Harhoff, "Technology Policy for a World of Skew-Distributed Outcomes," *Research Policy* 29 (2000): 559–66.

27. National Research Council, *A Patent System for the 21st Century* (Washington, D.C.: National Academies Press, 2004).

28. S. M. Maurer, A. Rai, and A. Sali, "Finding Cures for Tropical Diseases: Is Open Source an Answer?" (1994), http://salilab.org/pdf/136_MaurerBIOESSAYS2004.pdf.

Index

About the Authors

Dan L. Burk is the Oppenheimer, Wolff & Donnelly Professor of Law at the University of Minnesota Law School, where he teaches courses in copyright, patent, and biotechnology law. Professor Burk is the author of numerous papers on the legal and societal impact of new technologies, including articles on scientific misconduct, the regulation of biotechnology, and the intellectual property implications of global computer networks. Prior to joining the faculty at University of Minnesota, Professor Burk taught at Seton Hall University in Newark, New Jersey. He has also taught as a visitor at numerous other institutions, including Cornell University, the University of California–Berkeley, the University of Toronto Faculty of Law, George Mason University, Cardozo Law School, the University of Tilburg, and the Universita Cattolica del Sacro Cuore. Professor Burk is active in public service and has served as a legal adviser to a variety of private, governmental, and intergovernmental organizations.

Iain M. Cockburn is professor of finance and economics and Everett W. Lord Distinguished Faculty Scholar in the School of Management at Boston University, where he teaches and conducts research in business strategy, intellectual property, economics of innovation, and management of high technology companies. Prior to coming to BU, he was the VanDusen Professor of Business Administration in the Faculty of Commerce at the University of British Columbia. He is also a research associate at the National Bureau of Economic Research in Cambridge, Massachusetts. Professor Cockburn is published widely in leading journals in economics and management. Among his most widely cited papers are "Measuring Competence: Exploring Firm Effects in Pharmaceutical Research" in *Strategic Management Journal*, "Generics and New Goods in Pharmaceutical Price Indexes" in *American Economic Review*, "Racing to Invest? The Dynamics of Competition in Ethical Drug Discovery" in the *Journal of Economics and Management Strategy*, "Absorptive Capacity, Coauthoring Behavior, and the Organization of Research in Drug Discovery" in the *Journal of Industrial Economics*, and "The Changing Structure of the Pharmaceutical Industry" in *Health Affairs*.

Wesley M. Cohen is Frederick C. Joerg Professor of Business Administration and Professor of Economics and Management in the Fuqua School of Business, Duke University. He is also a Research Associate of the National Bureau of Economic Research. His teaching career includes twenty years at Carnegie Mellon University and courses covering economics of technological change, industrial organization economics, the economics of entrepreneurship, policy analysis, organizational behavior, corporate strategy, and the management of intellectual capital. Professor Cohen's research has focused on the economics of technological change and R & D. He has examined the links between firm size, market structure and innovation, firm learning, the determinants of innovative activity across industries and firms, the knowledge flows affecting innovation, the means that firms use to protect their intellectual property (especially patents), and the links between university research and industrial R & D. He has published in numerous scholarly journals and co-edited the recently published volume, *Patents in the Knowledge-Based Economy*. He served for five years as a main editor for *Research Policy* and served both on the National Academies' Committee on Intellectual Property Rights in the Knowledge-Based Economy and on the National Academies' Panel on Research and Development Statistics at the National Science Foundation.

Stuart J. H. Graham, JD, PhD, is assistant professor of strategic management in the College of Management at the Georgia Institute of Technology, where he teaches courses in law and international management. Professor Graham has written on intellectual property and litigation strategies in the software and biotechnology industries, comparative studies of the U.S. and European patent systems, and the use by companies of patenting and secrecy in their innovation strategies. Some of his recent publications include "Prospects for Improving U.S. Patent Quality via Post-Grant Opposition" in *National Bureau for Economic Research, Innovation Policy and the Economy IV* (with B. H. Hall, D. Harhoff, and D.C.

Mowery), "Submarines in Software? Continuations in U.S. Software Patenting in the 1980s and 1990s" in *Economics of Innovation and New Technology* (with D. C. Mowery), and "Intellectual Property Protection in the U.S. Software Industry" in National Research Council, *Patents in the Knowledge-Based Economy* (with D. C. Mowery). He is also an attorney licensed to practice in New York State and a member of the American Bar Association and the American Intellectual Property Law Association.

Robert W. Hahn is cofounder and executive director of the AEI-Brookings Joint Center and a resident scholar at the American Enterprise Institute. Previously, he worked for the Council of Economic Advisers. He also has served on the faculties of Harvard University and Carnegie Mellon University. Mr. Hahn frequently contributes to leading scholarly journals and general-interest periodicals, including the *American Economic Review, Yale Law Journal, Science,* and the *New York Times*. He is the author of *Reviving Regulatory Reform: A Global Perspective* and *In Defense of the Economic Analysis of Regulation*. In addition, Mr. Hahn is cofounder of the Community Preparatory School—an inner-city middle school in Providence, Rhode Island, that provides opportunities for disadvantaged youth to achieve their full potential.

Mark A. Lemley is the William H. Neukom Professor of Law at Stanford Law School, and the director of the Stanford Center for Law, Science and Technology. He teaches intellectual property, computer and Internet law, patent law, and antitrust. He is of counsel to the law firm of Keker & Van Nest, where he litigates and counsels clients in the areas of antitrust, intellectual property, and computer law. He is the author of six books and 57 articles on these and related subjects, including the two-volume treatise *IP and Antitrust*. Professor Lemley received his Juris Doctor degree from Boalt Hall School of Law at the University of California–Berkeley, and his Bachelor of Arts degree from Stanford University. After graduating from law school, he served as a law clerk to Judge Dorothy Nelson on the United States Court of Appeals for the Ninth Circuit, and practiced law in Silicon Valley with Brown & Bain and with Fish & Richardson. Before joining the Stanford faculty in 2004, he held the Elizabeth Josslyn Boalt Chair in Law at the Boalt Hall School of Law, University of California–Berkeley. Until January 2000, he was the Marrs McLean Professor of Law at the University of Texas School of Law.

David C. Mowery is William A. and Betty H. Hasler Professor of New Enterprise Development at the Walter A. Haas School of Business at the University of California–Berkeley, and a research associate of the National Bureau of Economic Research. Professor Mowery spent the 2003–4 academic year as the Marvin Bower Fellow at the Harvard Business School. He has also taught at Carnegie Mellon University, served as the study director for the Panel on Technology and Employment of the National Academy of Sciences, and served in the Office of the United States Trade Representative as a Council on Foreign Relations International Affairs Fellow. His research deals with the economics of technological innovation and the effects of public policies on innovation. In addition to serving on a number of National Research Council panels, he has testified before congressional committees and served as an adviser for the Organization for Economic Cooperation and Development. Professor Mowery has been published in numerous academic papers and has written or edited a number of books, including recent contributions: *Ivory Tower and Industrial Innovation; Paths of Innovation: Technological Change in 20th-Century America; U.S. Industry in 2000*; and *The Sources of Industrial Leadership*. His academic awards include the Raymond Vernon Prize from the Association for Public Policy Analysis and Management, the Economic History Association's Fritz Redlich Prize, the *Business History Review*'s Newcomen Prize, and the Cheit Outstanding Teaching Award.

Arti K. Rai is a professor of law at Duke University School of Law. In the fall of 2004, she was a visiting professor at Yale Law School. Her teaching and research interests include intellectual property (with a focus on patent law), law and the biopharmaceutical industry, and health care regulation. Her most recent publications include "Engaging Facts and Policy: A Multi-Institutional Approach to Patent System Reform," in *Columbia Law Review*; "Gene Patenting: A Case Study in Patenting Research Tools," in *Academic Medicine*; and *Law and the Mental Health System*, 4th edition (with Ralph Reisner and Chris Slobogin). Prior to joining the Duke Law faculty in 2003, Professor Rai was on the faculty of the University of Pennsylvania Law School, where she was also a visiting professor in the fall of 2000. She is on the board of editors of the *American Journal of Law and Medicine*, the advisory board for the Public Patent Foundation, and has served as a consultant to the National Human Genome Research Institute's ELSI program and to the National Academy of Sciences.

JOINT CENTER